River Ratting

Paul
Many thanks for your help with Ratting!

best, Nicholas Ford

'A brilliant evocation of the joys, delights and happy re-discoveries that come to friends who dare travel back into the many worlds of nature and landscape that so many of us lose sight of. A wonderful and inspiring read that will get you (like Ratty himself) travelling Beyond…'

William Horwood, Author

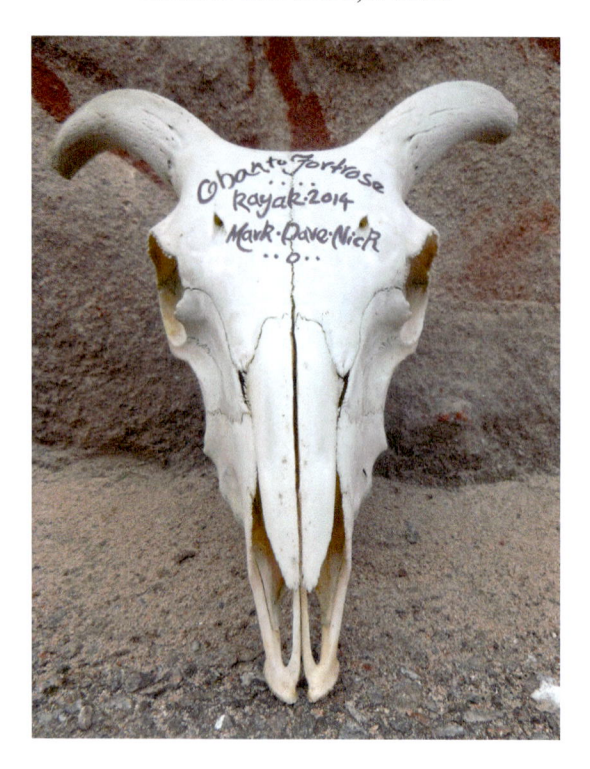

'River Ratting *flows like a good book should at a leisurely enough pace for the reader to reflect and appreciate their surroundings, both the natural world and the built environment. Nick Ford has a painter's eye for detail and a taste for tremendous trivia that puts Michael Caine to shame. I vicariously enjoyed the thrill of navigating unpredictable rivers and the open sea in the company of the author and his resilient, resourceful friends.'

Martin Doyle, Books Editor, *The Irish Times*

'The 'Rats' play well off each other with great humour. There are eye-opening encounters with wildlife and a strong literary side invoking the work of Roger Deakin, Peter Ackroyd and Robert Macfarlane.'

Paul Clements, Author and Journalist

River Ratting

Nick Ford

MOAT SOLE PUBLISHING

17 Wheelwrights Way, Eastry, Sandwich, Kent CT13 0JT

Copyright © 2025 by Nick Ford. All rights reserved

The moral right of the author has been asserted.
A CIP catalogue record for this book is available from The British Library

ISBN: 978-1-3999-9998-4

First Edition: 2025

Cover art by Hannah Firmin
Cartoons by Dave Chisholm FRGS
Editing and proofreading by Gilly Fisher
Layout by Bill Bond

This book is sold subject to the condition that it shall not, by way of trade or otherwise be lent, resold, hired out, or otherwise circulated without the publisher's prior consent in any form of binding or cover other than that in which it is published and without a similar condition, including this condition, being imposed upon the subsequent purchaser.

All photographs by the River Rats unless otherwise indicated.

Printed in the UK by 4edge Limited

ACKNOWLEDGEMENTS

Thanks to Dave and Bill Bond for their detailed work on the nuts and bolts of this, and to Hannah Firmin for creating the wonderful book cover.

Thanks to my family members and William Horwood, Martin Doyle, John Trotman, Paul Clements and Cat Horne, who kindly offered opinions or looked over some of this.

Thanks to Gilly Fisher for her methodical work in correcting all my errors.

Thanks to my wife, Kay, for her persistent support and acceptance that the home jobs list would deteriorate while I worked on this book.

Finally, deep appreciation to Dave and Mark for keeping the Rats afloat over the years, regardless of life's other complications.

PREFACE

We live in an ever-accelerating world where anxiety and frustration are commonplace. The kayak journeys that I have enjoyed over the years with my companions, Dave and Mark have always provided a time of deceleration and reflection. Setting out as the River Rats, I began to consider a simple message: we should accept things as they arrive and more deeply appreciate what is around us.

On a journey, the unexpected is to be expected. How you deal with obstacles to your progress and how you immerse yourself in your surroundings will depend on your perception of both. If you are accepting of change, then a challenge is perceived differently from if you perceive it as a problem that can't be solved. You can allow your environment to go by unnoticed or you can look, listen, feel, consider and fully experience. You can be enriched.

It was Dave who suggested that a written account of our kayak travels could be a worthwhile endeavour and he has created the fabulous cartoons that illustrate each chapter. Both Dave and Mark have also contributed to the script with their thoughts and observations.

War, poverty, climate change and the potential destabilisation of world order are great threats to nature. The more we can learn to understand the restorative character of the natural world, the more value will be placed upon its preservation.

This is a story of friendship and support. The three of us 'bimble' along together in our kayaks on the river or the sea. We live very closely together on the water throughout the day and when we pitch tent for the night the bond grows. We share tasks and obligations and an invisible understanding develops about who does what. We understand, with acceptance, each other's weaknesses and strengths.

Life is short, but life is wonderful. It will slip by us all, so we may as well fully embrace the good things.

TABLE OF CONTENTS

Chapter 1 - All For One   11

Chapter 2 - The Thames   15

Chapter 3 - The Wye   47

Chapter 4 - Scotland Coast To Coast   73

Chapter 5 - The Vjosa   109

Chapter 6 - London Town - August 2018   147

Chapter 7 - Pembrokeshire Coast   159

Chapter 8 - Medway   189

Chapter 9 - And One For All   201

About The Author   205

*To the warm friendship of my fellow River Rats, Dave and Mark:
great memories behind, great times ahead*

CHAPTER 1

ALL FOR ONE

A triangle is the strongest shape

A young river carries the fragile hopes of a vulnerable child. It emerges from the earth, pure and bright. It covers the early ground, shallow and eager. Its banks soon become more ordered and controlled. Bridges appear. Watercraft appear. Pollution takes its toll. Nothing, however, stops the flow. The river continues, gaining strength and developing character on the way. It takes its own imperfect journey.

The twists and turns, the white water, the still depths: each one is different. A river will always reach lower ground and eventually will spill, with stoic certainty, into the vast oceans.

One sunny spring morning, I approached my friend Dave in the car park of our children's school with the suggestion that we should kayak the length of the River Thames. He was immediately taken with the idea, but I'm not sure he had total confidence in my ability to keep us safe. We were again in the car park that afternoon and we wandered over to put the idea to another friend, Mark. We knew Mark to be highly experienced in climbing, and he had organised many expeditions, so with his equal enthusiasm, the triumvirate was established. This river journey was to become the first of many simple but glorious adventures that I was to share with these two middle-aged muckers.

Our time together was to bring me a connection with the world that often deserts us in the middle part of life, when commitments and obligations begin to weigh, and we lose sight of what it is to see the things around us with the wonder that we once did. Life is a series of journeys. A trip to my vegetable garden to pick radishes is a journey, but so too was my journey along worn vinyl flooring to kiss my dead mother goodbye. All journeys – both physical and mental – have unique meaning, and each journey will have many different destinations with discoveries along the way. I found that you don't have to travel to Mount Doom to discover a fantastical world. I was incredibly lucky. My choice of comrades turned out to be solid gold.

When we are navigating cross-country by water, engulfed in the natural world, or at the end of each day's paddling, on the wet grass under the pale fingernail moon of an evening sky, I can feel a connection between the three of us, to the impalpable entity of the river, and to the landscape around us. This is the thing that matters: the substance of this connection. It is the grounded energy that grows in children with hours of playing in the mud and the trees and the puddles. It is less than gas; it is not matter; but its content and meaning bring a tangible assurance to your place in a shifting world.

When we are young, there is little fear. Curiosity is still with us. We do things our own way and find our direction simply by having a go. Having a look. Our experiences are unpolluted with most of the rational thoughts and learned ideas that we all acquire as we grow. We observe things with clarity. Our paddling journeys together helped me rediscover this innocence and it became a renaissance.

A group of three engenders a spirit of action. Three musketeers, three little pigs, three stooges, three blind mice, three men in a boat. There are plenty of threes. In construction work, a triangle is favourite among architects. The triangle is the strongest shape. It will support itself better than any other. It is extremely stable. We called ourselves the River Rats, and we struck out as a team of three. And it has been that way since the start.

The Rule of Three

Mark's account of why a team of three is successful:

- *With two, you are fast and close, but in emergencies you quickly run out of help.*
- *With four, you can evolve into two pairs, rather than keeping as one team.*
- *More than four and things slow down. There will be a tendency to create a hierarchy.*
- *With three, it's possible to leave one person feeling left out. But it's easier to be egalitarian than with larger numbers, and three has the benefit of all inputs and equal support.*
- *There are three skills and three viewpoints without the drift apart into smaller groups or the top-down decisions likely with greater numbers. If one person is having a low day, with three, the others will spot this quickly.*

CHAPTER 2

THE THAMES

With a slower pace of travel, you more quickly find yourself far from home

It was a four-hour drive to Castle Eaton in Wiltshire where we River Rats spent our first night on a campsite. Cotswold villages are often inhabited by celebrities, or are weekend retreats for the privileged. The villages can sometimes seem very pleased with themselves. Castle Easton is modest and is not so smug.

We pitched camp and walked up to the Red Lion. We spent the evening recapping on our journey plan. We felt the freedom of being away, and the excitement of something new. We had no idea that this was the start of so many journeys together.

It was a small campsite – for tents only. There were only a few people staying and I had been chatting with a kindly looking, middle-aged Iranian man before we went out for the evening. In the morning, after a basic breakfast, I saw him kneeling in his small tent. I think he was at prayer, so I guess he was facing Mecca. He was on his own. After he'd finished praying, I started up a conversation again. He was living in that small tent and making a living by taxi driving in his own car. I wondered about what circumstances had led him to be living life in this way. I set him up to collect us from Teddington Lock as our return method to reunite with our vehicle once we had completed our journey.

We had a short drive to Cricklade, where we parked and brought our boats down to the water's edge next to the small bridge. We secured the Land Rover in a likely spot, where it would remain until we returned with the help of our Iranian friend.

The water levels were relatively high, so there was just enough draft to paddle from there. The Thames at this point is only one kayak's width, with thick vegetation and willow trees lining its banks. This was as close to the source as we could start.

The source of the river is a few miles further upstream, where a spring babbles its first life onto meadowland at Thames Head near Kemble in Gloucestershire.

We had an old, much-repaired white fibreglass double kayak, that Mark had acquired from a scout group. We knew it leaked a little. I had gone to the trouble of restoring a plywood and varnished single kayak that I had made at home when I was just twelve years old. I'd attempted a few sea trials, but the romantic idea

Thames Head
RIVER THAMES
14TH-19TH SEPTEMBER 2007
20-mile day
EYNSHAM
LECHLADE
Rushey Lock
START
CRICKLADE
Tadpole Bridge
ABINGDON
Benson Lock
WALLINGFORD
ONE FOR ALL
N
E
W
S
PANGBOURNE
22-mile day
READING
River Kennet
Dry bags
Snacks
THAMES
SNORE!
10
20
30
40
MILES

KINGFISHER
Dave Chisholm FRGS
S
NI
I
E
F
OXFORD
Iffley Lock
135 MILES
30-mile day
23-mile day
MARLOW
GORING
Hurley Lock
HENLEY
THE SULKER
MAIDENHEAD
Hampton Court
Tidal Thames
WINDSOR
STAINES
SUNBURY
FINISH
CHERTSEY
Teddington Lock
River Wey
LALEHAM
KINGSTON
LOCK
CAMP
27-mile day
13-mile day

of re-living adventures in the same craft of thirty-five years earlier was not going to float. It was too unstable and had no storage space. So we borrowed a very old fibreglass single kayak from a friend. And we had our three seats. We knew that the river was a tame one and we only had spray skirts for the double. Mark usually starts on any problem with the assumption that he can make do himself, so he had made a simple improvised tarpaulin sheet that we could tie over the exposed cockpit in the single. We hadn't invested in expensive bespoke kit and clothing. It was all a case of using what we had available.

The weather was good: no rain, warm with some sun. We clambered awkwardly into our boats and steadied ourselves as best we could. The first few paddle strokes quickly settled us down as we realised that the water was just deep enough for us to float. As it was so shallow, we had Mark, the lightest of us by far, in the double with Dave, and I had first shift in the single. We were to continually swap this combination around as we progressed.

None of us knew how this was all going to turn out, but I could recognise on our faces the optimistic anticipation of something special. We were concentrating on what we were doing to the exclusion of all else.

We were immediately and obviously within a different world. The water was slow-moving and clear. The flowing locks of vibrant river weed over the gritty riverbed swayed silent and lithe, like sidewinding snakes across sand. The charmer's flute sounded constantly as the breeze found melody through the alders. The reflected sunlight was shimmering on the wet grassy banks in conversation with the twitching leaves of aspen and willow. Nothing was said. We were underway.

✻

There had recently been some heavy storms. Signs of flooding were all around. The very narrow parts of this early section were strewn with trees that had fallen, and they spanned from bank to bank. Picking our way through, bending very low, or parting branches and debris to make our way, made the latter part of the morning seem easy-going and free. On later journeys, we also found this untidy tangle of vegetation –on the Arun and other rivers – in their early stretches. It's always a bit of a slog.

There were small timber platforms placed around a few lengths of river, which, we knew from signage, had been put there to encourage water voles. It was good to be alongside genuine river rats. Otters have also made a comeback, but they are elusive, and we were not lucky enough to see any.

We were soon at a point where the small river is joined by two tributaries, the Churn and the Coln. From here on, larger vessels can navigate. Historically, this was the upper limit for barges to carry agricultural produce to London. Today, it is the upper limit of motorised leisure vessels.

St John's Lock was our first. It is the furthest upstream lock on the Thames. At some locks we were able to join other boats in the enclosed pound between the heavy timber gates, so avoiding portaging. We had to carry at this manually operated lock. It never became a problem: each lock has an exit and entry point for canoes. Our boats, fully laden, and being of old-fashioned fibreglass construction, are a heavy lift with the toggle grips fore and aft digging uncomfortably into our palms. With two boats at each portage, only one of us had to carry twice.

There is a sculpture here of Old Father Thames. It was commissioned by Paxton for the Great Exhibition of 1851, where it was placed in a fountain basin at the Crystal Palace. It has been relocated over the years and was at Thames Head before being placed here in 1974. The statue, reclining in Henry Moore fashion and carved from Portland stone, is the work of Raffaelle Monti. There are no classical reference points or suitable landscape nearby to make sense of its location. He's not comfortable in his surroundings here.

Rivers everywhere, bringers of life, have long been associated with deities. The origins of Old Father Thames, depicted here with locks and beard like the flowing river itself, are certainly ancient, but they are also ambiguous. His likeness appears in different forms along the course of the river and through London.

We passed small Gloucestershire villages and a few farms. The building stone began to change a little in colour. The honey-coloured Cotswold limestone varies – from the darker umber hue against the pervading bleached ochre to a pale cream version.

All vernacular architecture has a belonging to location that is lacking in most development in the last century. This century is slightly better, but the ubiquitous cut-and-paste developments of monster cottage style – of brick and painted pine with plenty of UPVC – is depressingly familiar. A collection of buildings, even when built over many centuries, can feel like they grew from the earth, or that they belong to the landscape, so long as local materials dominate. This is true even on a large scale, for example, the locally baked clay tiles on a huge medieval barn, or the towering magnificence of the Bagshot Heath stone of Windsor Castle.

We admired Halfpenny Bridge as we continued through Lechlade. It is an attractive bow-backed limestone bridge with a toll house that displays a feeling of connectedness. Presumably, the toll was, at one time, a halfpenny.

We had now finished with Wiltshire to the south. Berkshire was now on our south side, with Oxfordshire replacing Gloucestershire to the north.

We paddled past William Morris' Cotswold retreat, Kelmscott Manor. This collection of buildings offers the same charm and feeling of belonging to its location. William Morris wrote about its natural harmonious setting. Few people have continued to influence taste and design as profoundly as Morris, and much of his inspiration is right here. He adored the countryside in this vicinity, much of which would be familiar to him now. I have visited the Red House at Bexleyheath, Morris's more famous home, the dreary built-up environs, which Morris would certainly not now recognise.

We were noticing more evidence of the recent flooding. We saw raised on a bank, at least a metre above the river level, a 30-metre-long barge, stranded on dry land like Noah's ark. It would be a tricky job to return it to service without breaking its back.

The river was gaining stature as it widened and deepened. The flow remained stately and we glided comfortably. We pulled up at a small boatyard to brew tea. Boatyards are usually scruffy, interesting places, and this was no exception. There is a camaraderie among people on the river. Barge dwellers, leisure boat operators, lock keepers, the rowing fraternity and so on, tend to support each other. Relationships with anglers are not always as cordial. We had already experienced less-than-friendly encounters with fisherfolk, who sometimes think that what they do is of more importance than floating along in a boat.

Dave took up discussion with a family group milling around, presumably while their boat was being repaired. Like many families, they had learned the pleasure of messing about with boats. The sun was now beaming. The tea was refreshing. We felt unhurried.

Paddling uses muscles that you might not exercise so often, and Dave was suffering from an aching arse. He rubbed his behind vigorously while moaning about the pain. Mark is small and agile. He is a very high-level judo competitor, so he is also strong and well-coordinated with good balance. His kayak entries and exits were good from the start. During this early trip, Dave and I hadn't yet mastered the best way to get in and out of the kayaks. It was quite a drop from any wharf that we had tied up against. It was my turn in the single. I stepped down with one leg into the very middle of the cockpit, then brought the other leg in as I crouched down. This was not an elegant entry, and I was rocking and shifting my weight to compensate. I said that I was 'fucking useless at this,' Mark said he was surprised that I rated my ability so highly.

Back on the sun-spangled water, there were shoals of tiny fish around our boats in the shallows near the edge – disguised ... until a silver belly flashed upward. The flow took us easily onward. We kept reminding each other that we were to pass other vessels on the right, the port side. Later, this became the natural thing to do. It only needed to be a guide to us tiny craft. The river was quiet. There were a few small barges. And by the end of the day, we had only seen one or two motorised leisure boats with holiday makers on board. If a greeting of some sort was not exchanged when you passed any boat at all, it would be an odd thing. We commented on this over the day, thinking what an improvement it might be if a city's pavements were the same. It would, I suppose, make a walk along Oxford Street a torturously slow event.

Moorhens were ever-present, their black-satin livery as smart as a city suit. Their two-syllable call echoed from bank to bank at all times. There were the common duck species: heron and, of course, the stately swan.

Swan behaviour can seem menacing. If venturing too close, kayaks are a threat to their territory. A cob and a pen swan look similar. We disturbed a cob bird, who puffed out his feathers as he glided towards us, with his powerful foot paddle movement just visible under the surface.

He hissed loudly and I could see the water wake increase as he did his best to dominate us. This behaviour gave me a brief chill. No cygnets were present, and he soon gave up. Mark commented that a swan can break your arm. I reminded him that such a tired cliché would only come from the mouth of a dullard.

Swans have long been associated with beauty and grace. There are three species of swan in Britain, and mute swans are by far the most prolific. There are thousands on the Thames. When seen on water, in sunlight, the sculpturally pleasing aspect of the folded wings, which extend loosely above the body, like large cupping hands as if presenting an offering, trap light behind and among the feathers. This makes the core of the bird seem to glow with a translucent soft light. A swan has the radiance of an angel, and the assured stateliness of an ocean liner.

There are many hues of white, and each white elicits its own response. The white of the swan has no blue, unlike the white of an avocet or the brilliant white from a decorator's paint tin. It is a warm and inviting white, a colour of tenderness. It is transcending, and has purity, innocence, and spirituality – like the swaddling clothes of the nativity. The neck curves back from the rounded bosom of the creature to the calm landscape of its back in a manner that balances the overall form. The short downy feathers around the base of the neck and near the head have subtle nuances of golden yellows – like sparsely gilded highlights of a revered object. These secondary feathers can rise to thicken and strengthen the appearance if the bird is threatened. The solid orange beak projects from a black base, with black tip and nostrils, in a flattening curve, and is topped with a bulbous basal knob, whose size and texture is like the black truffle treasure of Alba. This knob is bigger in the cob than the pen and he is slightly larger in size. The tiny grey-blue eyes buried on either side of its arrogant head, by contrast, are cold and unforgiving.

The movement of a swan on water is confident and serene, and only adds more to its elegant poise. There is little comical about a swan, but they are one of the heaviest flying birds. At Windsor, we watched as groups of swans took flight. The take-offs and landings are a laboured affair, which look strained, inelegant and slapstick. The impressive length they need to gain lift remind me of a cricketing bowler in fresh whites taking an impossibly long run-up to deliver his ball. The whooshing sound of the wings in flight, as air squeezes around the large wing feathers of a group of swans, can be heard from a distance. And if you happen to be looking the wrong way, it can be a puzzling phenomenon. The outstretched necks of a flock of flying swans give them an eagerness, and pointed direction. Like a bird on a wire, the head keeps its position as the beating wings move the heavy body rhythmically. They are bottom feeders, so they tilt down into the water to graze on weed, with the axis around the middle of the body. Bottoms point to the sky in an endearing display, their grey-blue heavy paddling webbed feet flopping around awkwardly. Like all water birds they remain miraculously dry. They are fiercely territorial and will hiss aggressively like a cat if they are threatened or have cygnets to defend.

The countryside here is pleasant and green. They might have built Jerusalem here. We were now in Oxfordshire and had only a few miles to reach where we had planned to stop on our first day. It would be an easy twenty miles.

We approached Rushey Lock and weir with plenty of daylight remaining. Machinery, lock keeper's cottage and associated structures are all well preserved and carefully maintained. The weir gave a background rushing sound to the atmosphere once we had climbed out of our boats and started to look over the place. The cottage has been a retreat over the years for celebrities, including Errol Flynn and Douglas Fairbanks. We called on the lock keeper, an amiable old gent with a white handlebar moustache. He gave us a key to the campsite set aside for boating people. We were the only campers. Once settled, we had a wash and freshened up before heading over, by torchlight, a few hundred metres downstream to The Trout at Tadpole Bridge.

CHAPTER 2 — THE THAMES

We had the bite of wind and sun on our faces that sharpened the appetite. We stumbled through the door, aware that we were a little late to order food. But Dave is a handsome man, with a persuasive smile in his eyes and broad chin. He put on his absolute best charm to the Eastern European waitress to ensure we were served. Like most pubs, it is much more feeding ground than watering hole. And a bit too smart for us travelling folk. Mark tried to enthuse us with a game of cards, but Dave and I could not maintain our interest. Dave said he may as well play with himself. 'No change there then,' I snorted, hysterical at my own weak joke.

Mark said that he appreciated the double entendre, adding, 'It's always good to slip one in,' The hot pies were quickly demolished.

We had discovered on the previous night that Dave is a world-class snorer, and, obviously aware of this, he had made a safe distance between us. This habit stuck on all our trips, by necessity. Mark and I shared a small tent, while Dave slunk off to seek shelter against a distant shed in his puffy bivvy bag like an old walrus cast out of the herd.

※

Setting off early in the morning, we slipped onto the calm water, fortified by tea and bacon. It was a glassy surface, with the dawn mist gently rolling in threaded curls, thickening at the banks. The familiar call of the ubiquitous coot carried across the flat surface. Almost immediately, we were startled in this torpid air by the surreal flashing turquoise shard of a kingfisher. It is an encouragingly common sight along the entire length of the Thames. We were to see them even among the tawdry urban graffiti at Maidenhead and Reading.

A master of wit can lift a conversation and create interest and humour by the clever juxtaposition of incongruous ideas. The kingfisher with the distinctive orange shade of its breast, the hue of which is perfectly complementary to the shocking electric blue of its body, is a scheme that would look more at home on the Amazon. It, too, elicits surprise and delight with its incongruity. Only a dolt, with no romance in his soul, would fail to be drawn to this bird.

It is not just the colours that appeal. The architecture of its exquisite miniature form – if you creep up close or can fix on it through a lens – is part pterodactyl and part slick fifties technicolour film star, with the dashing looks of a bygone age.

To really understand this bird, you must know of its habits. A sighting would often follow a repeated pattern. One of us would attempt to follow the bird, in our craft, into the willow branches where it first disappeared. Once we got close, she would dart away with rapid wing movement, flying close to the water, and settle again 20 metres or so further along the bank. We could not resist again approaching the bird until she again diverted downstream. This behaviour repeated.

In order to nest, Kingfishers burrow tunnels up to a metre into the riverbank. These are clear of vegetation and half a metre down from the top of a vertical bank. I've seen this in action. The mining birds never become dirty. They always emerge immaculately dressed. I've seen – when we kayaked down the Vjosa in Albania – how – in the filth and shabbiness of a poverty-stricken rural village, with muddy roads and concrete buildings where rusty rebar is visible in structurally suspect fissures – schoolchildren of proud matriarchs emerge from their homes in perfectly white shirts and blouses and well-pressed brightly coloured cotton blazers.

In their domain, the kingfisher is an ace predator, diving with precision into the water to spear its tiny prey, like some highly-polished lethal ninja weapon. There are few creatures anywhere, bird or beast, to match their unquestioned beauty.

The temperature was warming up. The river here is about 40 metres wide and has almost zero flow. This is a serene, pastoral part of the Thames. The smell was earthy. The river looked black, but was transparent and clear when looking straight down to the riverbed. Fish were usually visible, and river weeds sway at all depths. We came to call the kind of progress we were into here 'bimbling'. It was steady, meditative, and quiet. Views to absorb but not to discuss. Thoughts to ourselves. Paddle action on automatic. Almost a workmanlike approach to taking it easy. Bimbling, for us, has come to mean more than the OED definition, which is 'to walk at a leisurely pace'. It was to become very important to us over the years that followed. If we all spent more time bimbling, we would all be more content.

Bimbling

Mark's diary description of bimbling:

Water bimbling is messing about in boats while going somewhere. Access to a timepiece must be denied. Ambitious intentions and blood pressure are lowered.

⁂

We stopped at a gravelly section of bank to swap positions. It was my turn in the single. We sat in the ever-warming sunshine, squinting against the glinting river. The last of the year's yellow irises were intermingled with the reeds on the bank. We had seen the frothy white blooms of meadowsweet earlier in the river, but here we were rewarded with the white trimmed reddish heads of hemp agrimony, which I have always known as raspberries and cream. The real joy of this spot was the profusion of dragonflies and damselflies, endlessly staccato darting and stopping like military drones on active service.

Like Heinz varieties, there are fifty-seven species of dragonfly in Britain. The dragonfly is one of the earliest flying creatures on earth and there is a fossil-like hint in their appearance. The go-to place for information on these astonishing insects is the British Dragonfly Society. We were here looking at the bulkiest of them all, the emperor dragonfly. The colours of these iridescent beasts are remarkable. Many have the livery of an expensive car, with the burnished finish of metallic paint, ready for the showroom. The abdomen of the male emperor is blue, and the female's is green. The colours are precious, like turquoise and malachite respectively. They have outsized multifaceted compound eyes that have their own jewel-like quality. Their form is sculpturally arresting, with a colour-defined selection of black-outlined segments arranged in a variety of strange forms. There is also the scorpion-like rear end, giving a more helicopter than drone appearance. It is even more stimulating to the eye if you have the opportunity, when they finally rest, to admire the stained-glass look of the two sets of transparent veined wings. The microstructure of these wings possesses noise-reducing properties and their flight is silent.

Unsurprisingly, dragonflies are steeped in legend and folklore in many countries of the world and are usually linked with the devil or malevolent spirits. In England they are 'the Devil's darning needle' or 'ear cutter'. In Wales, they are 'the adder's servant'. In Germany, they are 'the Devil's horse'. And in Sweden, they weigh your soul in judgement and are an omen of tragedy. There are also superstitions concerning these striking-looking insects in Japan, Indonesia, and North America.

One aspect of these dark myths that stands out, is that they 'sew up the eyelids of liars'. A little further downriver, at a place where members cannot, by tradition, accuse each other of lying, the House of Commons, we could release a few. The members would be leaving the chamber, arms on the shoulders of each MP in front, like Pieter Bruegel's, *The Blind Leading the Blind*.

We had found that the single boat, an older build and design, was slower than the two-paddle power of the double. The single occupant ends up on his own, behind. This is Dave's explanation:

This was an ideal boat for me to enjoy my first strokes alone on the river. Initially, I had no control, but I soon settled into a rhythm and progress. As the days passed, and as we periodically rotated positions in the boats, it became apparent that the blue single was slower than the double. It soon fell behind. If the double had wing mirrors, the dual paddlers could have watched as the lone paddler slipped away into the distance, working harder than the other two and sulking. We called it **The Sulker** *and the name stuck!*

※

The river soon follows a northward loop around wooded hills at Wytham, and Cumnor. There is a stream leading to the mill where the fine paper for Oxford University Press was made for three hundred years until 1943. We were nearing Oxford.

This was to be our first encounter with 'Diamond Geezer'. He has a small narrowboat, and we were acknowledged as he overtook us. We came across him a few times again downriver. Our later encounters convinced me that he is an acid bath murderer with untold gruesome secrets in the bowels of his colourfully decorated canal barge.

Oxford crept up on either side of us. There were flat-bottomed punts, barges, skiffs, more leisure boats, and the first of many rowing eights. Tourists and students lined the towpath and banks. Sun hats and ice cream rubbed up against noble houses of ancient learning. Boat hire is as visible as dreaming spires. The architectural treasures of the Oxford colleges are many, but a detour into Oxford Canal or the Cherwell would have offered the best views. We stuck to the Thames proper, which, in Oxford, is usually called the River Isis.

We were not at all out of place with our wet trunks and T-shirts when we tied up at a mooring at The Head of The River pub in the centre of the city. We sat back in the riverside beer garden and enjoyed a rest and food among the throngs of people. 'It's not big and it's not clever,' I told Dave as he showed that he could grip a sausage between his nose and his upper lip.

The University is the oldest in the English-speaking world, usually acknowledged to start from 1096. It has dominated the town so fully since the twelfth century that other aspects of the town are easily forgotten. Motor manufacturing was successful here, starting with Morris, in 1910, which diminished as Britain's manufacturing base dwindled in the 1970s and 1980s. The Mini is still made at Cowley but is now German owned. Oxford has, in more recent decades, benefitted from the boom in IT industries. From our river view, however, we could only see the history of lofty education. The architecture spans many centuries. Everywhere you look – walls, pillars, finials, balustrades and every architectural adornment – there is the warm sandy glow of Cotswold stone.

On our way again and we were becoming aware of how much rowing, and boat clubs, dominate the Thames in Oxford. Most colleges have their own boat club, and there are forty in total in the town. They appeared frequently on both banks. Rowing eights, fours, and pairs were out in the afternoon sunshine, with seriously fit athletes on the water, working with precise rhythmic action, the larger of whom were under guidance from a diminutive cox. Sculling is big in Oxford. The entire length of the Thames has boat clubs. There are over one hundred of them.

As a sleek sculling four powered past us, Dave commented that they made a first-class spectacle. 'Minimum upper-middle,' I pointed out. The manicured lawns of the colleges had instructed us to 'Keep Off The Grass', but it felt more appropriate to 'Keep Off The Class'. The major public schools have traditionally fed talent into the sport, and Eton College, downriver, hosted the rowing events for the 2012 Olympic Games. It has been said that Britain excels at the sitting-down disciplines, and rowing is a prime example. It's not all toffs and privilege in the rowing world, however, as Windsor Boys' School, a state school, also downriver, is one of the most successful junior rowing clubs – and rowing Olympians come from all backgrounds.

The boat clubs usually have broad stone or concrete steps leading into the water from the boathouses, like partially submerged Aztec temples. The shapely, fit young rowers – of both sexes – busy with their boats on these steps, turned our heads, and we received warm smiles in return.

The afternoon was moving on, and we wanted to reach Abingdon that evening – another ten miles. We were in a landscape now whose fertile ground has long supported human habitation. Abingdon has been a settlement for at least six thousand years and is one of Britain's oldest towns. The course of the river appears established and natural, but every aspect of our surroundings has the touch of man. There is nothing wild here. The many locks, drainage, and other water controls tame and contain the natural forces of the river. We put heads down and paddled on into the early dusk.

We found a spot near Abingdon Lock with long soft grass on flat ground. The dew had already saturated everything, so we remained wet. We made camp speedily.

We took a short walk over the lock bridge to the nearest hostelry where we immediately retreated to the gents and took turns drying off and warming under the hand dryer. We directed the hot air over our hair, down our trousers and shirts, luxuriating in a hot air shower. It had been a thirty-mile day. As is often the case, one side of the pub was lively and loud, the other side was full of dull couples out together: a place where conversation has gone off to die. By the end of a short evening, we had the weary, satisfied glow that comes with comfort after a day's exertion.

I am usually the first up and busy in the day, so I often make the breakfast. I brewed tea for us all. Mark is quick and sharp. He takes the tea with gratitude. Dave is more bull-like and phlegmatic. He will take the tea with equal gratitude, but will then doze off a few times.

The mist on the calm river once again provided a dramatic display. A pair of swans silently made their way through the vapour that gently billowed and expanded, like the dry ice on the stage of a Covent Garden opera production. Dew-dripping spiders' webs hung twinkling from twigs, and the grass was covered in a loose-weave carpet of a thousand horizontal webs. The dawn chorus provided the music, and watching Dave and Mark emerging from their sleeping bags, shaking themselves down, in pants and T-shirts, with the bright fuzz of hairs on their legs, backlit by the warming sun, provided an inelegant dance performance.

CHAPTER 2 — THE THAMES

There was a short carry for our boats to the other side of Abingdon Lock, then we were away. Our behaviour often mirrors what is around us, so we spoke with muffled voices in appreciation of the splendour of the morning.

During the many trips we were to make over the years, the special nature of travel by kayak was appreciated by all of us. The fluid nature of water means that when you are on a river, you will always be at the lowest point of your surroundings. You will, therefore, like a child, always be looking up. You are carried. There are gentle rhythmical movements and sounds that take you back to even before childhood. At the base of a rocky cliff or towering canyon, you can feel a paternal comfort from the landscape, or, if tying up against a soft grassy bank, you can begin to feel an unspoken understanding of Mother Nature. You become an observer of things around you and there is a return to the forgotten pleasures of long ago.

To fully savour your surroundings on a journey, you should remain unhurried and unsullied. You can passively observe the world and your feelings. There is a cleansing. You find yourself bimbling along without thoughts of the past or the future. You have no expectations and things are left to chance, accepting without judgement experiences as they happen. Time becomes less linear. There is a tendency to look for the quickest way to reach a destination, but with a slower pace of travel, you more quickly find yourself far from home.

The river twists a big curve eastward after Abingdon. The countryside remained largely flat with plenty of hedges, pastureland, and stubble fields. The river continued to feel heavier and more substantial, especially several miles on, once we had gone beyond the confluence of the Thame at Dorchester.

The origin of the name Thames has added dimension at this confluence. As with so much information offered to us from many sources, there are differing views on the origin of the name, but these views are usually expressed as if there is certainty in the writer's opinion. Clearly there is no certainty.

Most place names in the area here have Anglo Saxon origin and the endings are '-ing', '-folk', '-ford', '-ham', '-ton', and '-wich'. Thame is an older Celtic word. It may mean 'tranquil river', or it may mean 'dark river'. Rivers with this same root include the Tamar in Devon and Cornwall, another River Tame in Manchester, and the Teme in Worcester. All these areas had been Celtic-speaking until AD 500, at least. It is often put forward that the name 'Thames', or older 'Tamesis', is the union of the name 'Thame' and 'Isis', the Isis being the name of the river from source to this point. The link with this Egyptian goddess is also controversial, but it seems likely that the 1546 translation of 'Ysa' – one half of Thame and Ysa – as 'Isis' by the historian John Leland properly expanded this connection. Peter Ackroyd, in his *Thames: Sacred River*, puts the name in a broader international context: from very early times of wandering Mesolithic tribes, where he identifies the Sanskrit word tamasa, meaning 'dark', in the Tamasa, a tributary of the Ganges; the Temes in Hungary; the Tamese in Italy; and the Tamar here in England.

※

Wallingford is the next settlement as the river turns due south for a while. On the east bank, just after the beautiful stone bridge, there is a designated open-water swimming area that they call Wallingford Beach. It was before midday, but even though it was fine weather, there were just five or six swimmers splashing around. So-called 'wild swimming' has increased in popularity as our lives have become increasingly urban and reliant on technology. Waterways had begun to show improvements in cleanliness through the end of the last century, but as investment in the infrastructure has diminished in favour of dividends to shareholders and directors, the privatised water companies are discharging pollutants into our rivers at an unsustainable rate. Chemical runoff from intensive farming shows little sign of adequate containment.

Roger Deakin's *Waterlog: A Swimmer's Journey through Britain* was first published back in 1999, and narrates a delightful journey through the magic of all things watery in Britain, as he swam in every location and circumstance conceivable, and was influential among people in my own circles. The desire must be there for cleaner rivers, so with this will, let's hope there's a way.

Dave is part man, part sea mammal. He is a dedicated open-water swimmer. He has swum the English Channel and the 41 miles around Jersey – both solo. And he has also completed four English Channel and one length of Lake Geneva team relay swims. Dave is the wild swimmer among us three.

Wallingford was a new town created by Alfred the Great, King of Wessex, and the ninth-century road layout is unchanged. William the Conqueror, often referred to as William the Bastard, in 1066, took surrender here from Wigod, Lord of Wallingford and a Norman sympathiser. William's army could at last cross the Thames, and William officially took the throne of England. A massive castle was built, which, much later, was destroyed by Cromwell. The town had never fully recovered from the ravages of the Black Death. Three hundred years later and no great significance was ever to re-emerge.

We again came up against Diamond Geezer puttering along in the opposite direction. He recognised us from earlier, and greeted our party with a doff of his floppy white cricket cap.

CHAPTER 2 THE THAMES

I had read a little about Moulsford Railway Bridge, which was our next feature over the river. Dave and Mark made such a great display of huge yawning when I started on about the bridge, I thought they were going to try and eat the thing. It is one of three rail crossings built by the visionary giant of Victorian engineering, Isambard Kingdom Brunel, in the 1830s. The Maidenhead crossing, which we would later paddle through, is the most famous because of the extremely flat arches and the spectacular echo created under the so-called 'sounding arch'. Apart from its innovative, lightweight design, Moulsford Railway Bridge is unusual because it crosses the river at sixty degrees. It is a 'skew bridge'. A second bridge has now been added. Brunel's bridges were part of his scheme to create a seamless journey from London to New York, setting off at Paddington, alighting from a train at Temple Meads in Bristol, then boarding Brunel's *SS Great Britain* steamer, the world's first ocean liner, at Bristol Docks, to then cruise to New York. The world now seems lacking in this kind of huge visionary idea.

Mark commented on the twisted brick construction of each of the four shallow arches, only truly visible from the water, where the bricks are laid at a forty-five-degree angle, and not parallel to the sides of the bridge. You can feel, just by the look of it, how the cross-tension construction is made stronger with this method. I pointed out to Mark that Brunel was a short-arse like himself and only five feet tall. Brunel's habit of wearing a huge stove pipe hat is an image that perfectly symbolises the Industrial Age in the most obvious way. I suggested that Mark should buy one so he could feel important and tall. Height jokes are never going to ruffle Mark.

The river traffic remained quite light, and we continued to have the river to ourselves. We pulled up a couple of times on the stretch to Goring and Streatley, to swap seats and to brew tea, and snack on nuts and biscuits. We were at the southern end of the Chiltern Hills, whose chalk soil and landscape, as a man of Kent, living on the Downs, was familiar to me. At Goring Lock, we filled up containers with water and settled for a lunch break.

The weir here runs to an island under Goring Bridge and then another weir goes from there to the Streatley bank. Everything was gradually beginning to increase in scale: the locks, the weirs, the boats – even the middle-class riverside dwellings. Both Goring and Streatley are separate villages, linked by a bridge, but are usually referred to as one place, like some comedy double act from the 1970s. Each village is in a different county, but the station, golf club, tourist information etc. are all known as Goring and Streatley.

On the south side are the Berkshire Downs, and the Thames channel between the two downland areas is known as Goring Gap. The views on both sides across Berkshire and Oxfordshire are gentle and pleasing. A thousand years ago, as a sixteen-year-old, I finished a walk along The Ridgeway path at this place. The route can now be traced quite easily much further northeast. Robert Macfarlane's *The Old Ways: A Journey on Foot*, includes much on this route, and the ongoing Icknield Way, in his inimitable, enlightening style.

There is a pervading tidiness to the area, like an idealised foreigner's view of the British countryside. Willow trees and country houses, quiet river, hedgerows and courtesy, all disguising hidden drama and tragedy. It looks like a wonderful place for a murder. I am sure we saw Miss Marple at the post office, and Conan Doyle's copper beeches swaying in the wind.

We had made a revised plan of each day's approximate distances with likely stop-offs. We planned to reach Pangbourne that night. We were slow to get underway after Goring, and what remained of the afternoon sped along quite quickly with the riverside charms and ease of the day bimbling into early evening.

※

There is a well-kept mown grass common on the bank at Pangbourne and we settled there for the night. As we walked away from our boats and one tent, collected neatly together near the water, we crossed the small common on our way into the village. We stepped over a sign facing the road, and not the river, which read 'Strictly No Camping'. Doesn't apply if approached from the river obviously. We slept tired and sound having enjoyed the evening plotting out the following day's journey plan over beer and hot food.

There is a white-painted iron bridge at Pangbourne. We all had a stretch of soon-to-be-cramped legs in the cool morning, so we walked to the middle of the bridge, looking into the dark river. It is called Whitchurch Bridge, and it joins two villages. The iron structure replaced a timber one in 1902. It has a tight lattice pattern to the decorative balustrade, and the shallow arch is supported by three sets of plain iron piers. The white-painted Victorian iron bridge, in its many decorative and engineered forms, was to become very familiar to us. We've seen them, each with their own different charms, as rail, foot, road, and livestock crossings, in all the rivers we have paddled. By Victorian standards, the structural and painted decoration is often relatively plain, but the use of iron and steel by this time was confident and no longer experimental. The appearances have an aesthetic quality beyond pure engineering function with simple adornment. Care is taken to achieve an overall balance. I do not understand why iron river bridges are almost always painted white. Bridges over rail and road are usually not white. It might be that white is equated with lightness and space, something less prominent in stone or timber bridges because they lack the strength to span as far as iron.

Pangbourne was the home of Kenneth Grahame. The inspiration for his books is right here. The river had not yet changed its overriding rural character, and as we paddled our way towards the large urban conurbation of Reading, six miles downriver, we could still hear the 'wind in the willows'. Mr Toad, Ratty, Mole, and Badger were never far away.

Reading displays expensive properties and here there are boat clubs, high-tech industry, modern infrastructure, privilege and wealth. There is also poverty and litter, under-education and graffiti. There was a travellers' camp on an area of the north bank, with a collection of old fridges, bicycles and waste blighting their environment. At this time there were no official travellers' sites in the city.

The two Thames road bridges in the town, Reading Bridge and Caversham Bridge, are not inelegant, but they are the first crossings of metropolitan character and scale. There is now a pedestrian bridge, Christchurch Bridge, connecting Reading to Caversham. I have since visited and walked across this structure. It is called a cable-stayed bridge, being supported by fourteen pairs of cables from a 39-metre mast. The mast supports the curved span that is not central, creating a tension in appearance. The programmed coloured lighting on and under the bridge is a poor choice and will soon look dated.

We pulled up to replenish supplies at a small mooring by a supermarket car park. I stayed with the boats and watched as several groups of rowers swept by, one after another, like 20-metre-long water-riding insects, chasing each other with synchronised feet. It had turned cold, so hot barbecued chicken was very welcome. We had our customary seat changes and Dave took *The Sulker* on the next leg. Rain came. Hats on, eyes squinted, shoulders hunched.

The River Kennet joins the Thames here. Dave gave us all a little history of the Devizes to Westminster canoe race, which emerges from the Kennet, in Devizes, into the Thames at this confluence.

Since 1948, the race – or marathon – is held every Easter. It is a 125-mile sprint, with no land team aid of any kind. Originally it was a challenge to see if the Devizes scout group could navigate through the part derelict Kennet and Avon Canal to the Thames and on to Westminster in less than one hundred hours, with all food and camping kit being carried in the boats. Interest boomed and it soon became dominated by the armed forces, using it as a training exercise. Except for in 1952, when teams from the Paras, the Royal Marines, and the SAS and Special

Forces won the event between 1951 and 1974. The race eventually became a non-stop competition for the elite teams, and the long-standing record, set by Brian Greenham and Tim Cornish, from Richmond and Reading Canoe Club respectively, was set in 1979 at the insane speed of 15 hours 34 minutes. A solo record of 14 hours and 46 minutes was set in 1993 by G Butler of Nottingham Kayak Club. DW medal owners include the politician Paddy Ashdown, the explorer Sir Ranulph Fiennes, Olympic gold medallists James Cracknell and Helen Glover, and the mountaineer Rebecca Stephens.

As younger men, we would have enjoyed the challenge. But it is no way to enjoy the river. Like serious summit scaling, the enjoyment of such action has little to do with the environment and more to do with yourself. As a team-building exercise, there would, however, be immense satisfaction in completing the course.

We portaged around Sonning Lock and were immediately through Sonning Bridge on the eastern side of Reading. The bridge is a return to cottage scale and design. This multiple-arched redbrick landmark is a much photographed and painted sight. Our mood relaxed as the tension, just visible through the town, began to dissipate. The rain stopped.

✼

The three of us continually comment on what is around us. We discuss what we are to expect next, and we make plans and adapt them as circumstances demand. Our actions are as fluid as the river. We had become accustomed to the procedure we were likely to follow at locks, so the conversation is confirmatory and decisions are quickly made.

The length of river between here and Marsh Lock at Henley is built-up, but the tranquillity is largely undiminished. The River Loddon tributary joins us at Wargrave. The occasional pleasure boat cruised by with friendly comment from the occupants; a few barges very slowly crept along at little more than our own paddling speed. We portaged around Shiplake Lock, then paused to chat and rest at Marsh Lock, Henley. The riverside properties were becoming grand.

Henley Bridge was badly damaged in 2010 when a sizeable pleasure boat crashed into it, which led to a major structural refurbishment. The name of the boat was *Crazy Love*. All of us have needed major attention, at some time or other, when this comes crashing without warning.

CHAPTER 2   THE THAMES

The stone bridge has five elliptical arches and a handsome balustrade. The consoles of the central arch are set with two bas-relief sculptures. These works were chiselled by Anne Seymour Damer in 1785 and depict the masks of Tamesis and Isis.

Isis is female and Tamesis is male. The Thames is represented here as a union of male and female deities. English has not treated its nouns as masculine or feminine since Anglo Saxon times, so a river has no grammatical gender. The word for 'river' in European languages seems to be masculine, but there is a complete mix with the names of each individual river. Over the channel, there is la Seine in France and also la Dordogne – both feminine. There is die Mosel (feminine) in Germany, but also, der Rhein (masculine). There are examples in other languages, not just European. The Indians see their sacred River Ganges to be feminine. Rivers everywhere have long been associated with deities or spirits, which must give some clue to the genders associated with any river. Isis is an ancient Egyptian goddess of fertility, the mother of Horus. Roman images of Horus have been found under London Bridge. Tamesis may have its name very far back in history but is a word used by the Celts, and in the representation over the river here, it is depicted as a male god, an image that is very like representations of Old Father Thames, which is first referenced in a poem by Alexander Pope in 1713. The name is like the male depiction of the Mississippi in Hammerstein's *'Ol' Man River'*, where the endless flow of the uncaring river is a metaphor for toil and hardship suffered by African Americans working there.

The Thames is unusual in that it has a mix of genders from other languages. It is, for example, feminine in French and German but is masculine in Portuguese and Italian. Some rivers with either gender flow into a river with a different gender. It is the same water, but its gender has changed. A river is nothing without water; it is just land, so it is not simply the landscape that gains a gender, it is the sum of the parts. The way we use language profoundly affects the way we see the world and will have bearing on the decisions and actions we choose. The debate around gender and how we act according to the way we identify ourselves and see others, and the world around us, has become increasingly important. Language has not caught up with these concepts. The river has both male and female attributes. It is not a living entity with a view of itself. It is up to us how we think of it as 'her' or refer to it as 'him'. It is a giver of life. It is nurturing. It can support you. It can caress you. The river is also assertive and dominating. It can be frightening and overpowering. It can take your life. It can also freeze over or divide endlessly and become gas. It can be whichever aspect we wish to focus upon.

RIVER RATTING

There is a naturally straight length of river, in a northerly direction, starting immediately downstream from Henley Bridge. This is ideal for the boat races. We had already seen the distinctive moorings of the Henley Rowing Club and the Leander Club. The Upper Thames Rowing Club is a little further on. Henley Royal Regatta has been and remains a social calendar must for many. It is a huge event. Henley hosts open-water swimming events, which are gaining popularity to complement the rowing events.

Dave gave us a little talk on the skills of sculling. There were pairs, fours and one eight, all in practice when we passed through. Sculling looks precarious. Muscle-bound athletes, often XXXL, perch-balanced on sliding seats on slender polished hulls with wide-reaching riggers, bracing exceptionally long, narrow oars. My wife, Kay, with a partner in Norwich, were a successful competing pair of scullers in their day; they called themselves '*the Norfolk Broads*'.

Watching the eight, Dave, whose alma mater had rowing teams, pointed out that, despite how it appears, each rower on his respective numbered seat has a slightly different job to execute. The crew exhibits ultimate teamwork. Each rower's tasks have only nuanced differences not at all visible to the spectator. Each rower is dependent on the others. The cox is key to success and only he is looking to the direction of travel. You must trust the cox so you are free to put your head down and concentrate. A hesitant or indecisive cox could mean that people could be injured, equipment could be damaged, and the race would be lost. Life is a team sport, but without effective leadership, we are all sunk. In our beaten-up old kayaks, loaded with all our kit, our weather-leathered tortoise necks craned to admire the hares fly by.

We were out of our kayaks for a while and Mark was chatting to a ruddy-faced rotund barge man, whose trousers were a bit too tight, and who seemed a bit too old to wear a baseball cap the wrong way around. He gave us tips for 'best camp'. The island at Hurley Lock would be best, so we had our target set.

The straight river and well-tended landscape, terminating at the spot regarded as the start of the regatta course, with the classical folly on Temple Island, was a unique experience to kayak. It was hard not to think of this as a racetrack.

Mark, in *The Sulker*, made a sudden dash to effect race mode. Dave and I were too fast for him. 'You are just not hard enough sonny,' we cried as we overtook with ease. Of all the people of note who live, or have lived, in Henley-on-Thames, the most unlikely must be Gerry Anderson, one of the creators of *Thunderbirds*. On telling the boys about this, Mark said that he was surprised to learn that he had settled outside Ireland and that he had no time for terrorists. Quickly realising Mark had assumed Adams not Anderson, Dave and I kept the thing going with talk of the Irish prowess in rowing and how the IRA had its own elite squad of scullers that trained in secret. When Mark finally had his memory restored, I warned him that Temple Island is, in truth, Tracy Island and that when the world comes calling, the trees lie flat, the dome of the folly folds back and *Thunderbird 1* emerges, with Scott Tracy wobbling around in the hot seat.

Once through Hambleden Lock, the river turns east, and narrowboats are frequent, often moored on the north bank. River islands on the Thames are known as eyots and we had skirted around many. These were appearing more frequently. We enjoyed a pleasant, if chilly, late afternoon bimble as far as Hurley Lock, where we found the lock keeper who gave us the key for the basic amenities, which were ideal for us. We had our own little island, a toilet, a shower, and our own key; this was utter luxury. We spread out untidily on the flat ground to dry off and set about minor repairs to the double, where we had a slow leak at the nose of the bow.

Mark had been keen to visit places or pubs visited by the *'Three Men in a Boat'*. So far, we had either missed them, found them far too gentrified for the likes of us dressed like tramps, or, like The Swan at Pangbourne, found the place shut for refurbishment. We quickly Googled that the central pub at Hurley was shut at that point, so Mark phoned somewhere a little out of the village to check, hoping to avoid a long walk, only to have expectation dashed at the end. By good fortune, the proprietor was most keen to have us visit. He told Mark that it was curry night and that he would happily collect us and bring us back to the river later. This was looking good. A youngish, very chatty man, in jeans and T-shirt, collected us in a shabby old car. When we arrived at his pub, we could see why he was eager for our meagre trade. Instead of the sound of tinkling glasses and the warm welcome of convivial hubbub, there was a yawning quiet, no heating, and the ghastly green hue of a neon strip light hung over a forlorn bleached bar billiard table. We would be the curry night. He was the only staff, and we were the only customers. *Hey-ho*, we thought. We could hear the ping of the microwave preparing our authentic Punjabi feast. There was signage around the place about it being wine o'clock, or the free beer given out tomorrow. The beer was OK and so too was the supermarket curry and we were glad to be sitting upright. We were happy and dry, and the place gave us permanent smirks. On the trip back, our enthusiastic landlord told us of his (unlikely sounding) big plans for his restaurant. He was not short of hope, but it looked desperate. Such a pleasant man to be around. Good luck to him.

That evening, Mark decided to read aloud to us from Jerome K Jerome's book. He had found a great chapter, and Mark and I allowed Dave into our tent for the recital. I laid back comfortably, Dave curled up on his side in his sleeping bag, and Mark sat up with folded legs as he recounted the stories of three other men paddling down the Thames together one hundred and twenty years earlier.

⨉

We had been spoiled by clear weather, and once again, the sun rose with the promise of warmth. This was our penultimate day on the water.

We were very soon at Temple Lock and weir. We were just starting to feel the pull of the metropolis. At each lock it felt that we had dropped another half metre or so closer to sea level. We were soon in Marlow. The twelfth-century All Saints Church on the south bank is a striking view because it is right up close to the river, with a mooring up to the massive tower. The huge stone structure seems too heavy and looks like it should sink into the river. Looking over any river tends to obscure the fact that a river is simply land with water on it. The depth of the water makes little difference and the concept of land is totally altered.

We paused on the water in Marlow to chat to a kindly lady who was on the river in a small rowing boat. She was crossing to do her shopping. We didn't have cameras on phones in those days. I had been using a small camera and needed a new memory card. I asked if she could help. She had one at her home. She rowed back to her riverside house and returned, meeting us on the other bank to give me the memory card. It was the wrong size, but I decided not to ask her to go back for another one and thanked her profusely. When people you've never met are so helpful, everything looks better. Whatever misery weighs within is immediately lightened.

I am a one-time resident of Bristol. I lived there in a flat with a view of Brunel's Clifton Suspension Bridge. It is such a stunningly dramatic bridge, and living there has left me unable to look impassively at any impressive bridge. I have even made a special journey to Southwest France to travel across the epic Millau Viaduct. I have walked across the Danube, from Buda to Pest and back again, across the magnificent Széchenyi Chain Bridge in Budapest. William Tierney Clark was a pioneer in suspension bridge design and his Hungarian bridge opened in 1849. The suspension bridge in Marlow is the earlier model of the large-scale replica built in Budapest.

Completed in 1832, it is, of course, painted white. The stone towers and looping steel cables supporting a gently curved thin road deck on heavy-duty vertical suspenders is appealing, in part, because it is engineering simplicity. The compression forces of the towers and the tension forces on the cables and suspenders are visible and easy to understand. All bridge design is the creation of a balance of forces. There are, of course, diverse designs around the world, but they all balance compressive forces in some places with tensile forces elsewhere, so there is no overall force to cause motion and do damage. Not all suspension bridges are wonders of the modern world. The Spanish, in sixteenth-century Peru, discovered hundreds of suspension bridges made of twisted grass that spanned up to 50 metres. As suspension bridges became much larger and more ambitious in the twentieth century, they were often located in windy estuaries; the song of the wind, like the opera singer and the glass, revealed that without careful aerodynamic design, torsion, the twisting force, could occasionally cause vibration at a rate known as resonance frequency. This could create wild movement, and, in some tragic cases, has ended in catastrophe.

On through Marlow, kites were often above us, wheeling and turning on their six-foot wingspan. Kites are now a common sight on the nearby M40. They eat mainly carrion, so roadkill is a draw for them, and they have the thermals over the tarmac to aid flight. It's hard to remember that they had vanished from our skies until just thirty years ago. They continue to increase their range and population numbers. They are one of only a few recent success stories of birds in Britain.

We were in light mood and Mark started singing tunelessly. Dave and I couldn't bring ourselves to shut down this expression of his delight, even at the expense of our own. I cannot sing, but like most of us blighted with dull voice and poor tuning, I will sing, but only alone in my car. Mark has no such reservation.

The riverbanks became very steep, with wooded cliffs and attractive overhanging branches skimming the water surface. The silhouette of Cliveden House spread across the horizon through a clearing in trees that looked as if Gainsborough had painted them. There is history associated with all great houses like this one, but in this case, the 1963 Profumo scandal will always trump any other association.

Turning south past Taplow, and into Maidenhead, I bored the boys with some Brunel talk as we were at Maidenhead Railway Bridge, with its startling sounding arch. At the time of construction, Brunel's associates would not believe that the innovative low-rise arches would be safe, so the centring was left in place. A year later, in 1839, this centring fell away in a storm, validating the design, as the bridge remained standing. Listening to the echo under the central arch, created by accident and not design, is truly remarkable. It is worth a visit just to experience this strange phenomenon. The echo could have been generated by a sound engineering workshop for a film, or for research. Hearing our voices sharply echoing repeatedly, outside, in real time, is irresistible, so we played around with different sounds for some time. The sound creates a kind of hypnotic comfort. It has a percussive quality, like shingle drawn back to the sea after a breaking wave. It is strange and ghostly.

We cruised under the M4 with just two or three miles to go before Windsor. The riverbanks were quiet and attractive, agriculture was on both sides, but we could feel the invisible weight of a busy world nearby. Heathrow launches a never-ending stream of aviation above; the M4 and the M25 nearby roar and breathe poison; the rumbling rail networks, reaching out from London like the claws of grasping hands pulling people to its bosom, were around us on all sides.

The ever-busier motorways are themselves like meandering rivers. They have their own dams and stagnation. Traffic has its own flow, and it has its own bank holiday flooding. The study of traffic flow is based on fluid dynamics, and wave theory is key to managing traffic. The Thames in Central London, when viewed from a nineteenth-century point of view, is like a deserted motorway. What use will these corridors of tarmac be put to should we all one day be free of individual vehicle traffic?

The Windsor Castle outline, dominated by the enormous cylindrical keep, rose on the south bank ahead. There was a flotilla of swans in substantial numbers. We stopped for a stretch. They have become quite used to the numerous tourists offering a steady diet of bread. Dave said they had appalling manners and were pushy and rude with too much confidence. They were pestering us like professional beggars. The swans were unmoved by our threats to 'up' them. We decided that the ambition to become one of the King's Swan Uppers was hilarious.

In July, travelling upriver as far as Abingdon, boatmen in splendid-looking skiffs, with smart colour-coordinated uniforms, flags fluttering at the bow, carry out the ceremony of counting, ringing and health checking the swans. This is known as swan upping. Historically, only the Crown can grant ownership of the nation's mute swans in any given body of water. There are two City of London livery companies that still exercise this right of ownership, the Vintners, and the Dyers' companies. They have their own swan uppers who take part in the ceremony, with associated officials, such as the Swan Marker. Historically, swans would be marked by the uppers nicking their beaks. There are several pubs with the name The Swan With Two Necks. This should read 'With Two Nicks'. The birds are surrounded by the skiffs, then captured to check for wellbeing, and if they are not ringed, the cygnets will be marked with their owner's ring. I doubt that poaching these graceful birds for food is a problem, but fishing tackle, line, and tiny weights are a hazard for them, so the ceremony retains a useful function. The ceremony dates back to the twelfth century, when swan was a dish reserved for only the most privileged tables. Henry III had forty swans presented at table for Christmas celebrations in 1247, with the roasted birds re-dressed in their skin and feathers, blazing incense in their beaks.

※

On through Windsor, with Eton and Eton College to the north. More notices: 'Keep Off The Grass'. The river loops around the mature landscape of Windsor Great Park, then dives south to Runnymede. We stopped for a brew behind a barge on a lengthy but quiet concrete mooring. A middle-aged man appeared from below deck at the rear of the barge. He wore oversized white shorts, and his shiny tracksuit top, emblazoned with an official logo of some rowing club, was zipped taut over a round paunch. His head was a bit too large for his body, and his face sported thick metal-rimmed glasses that distorted the size of his eyes. He had floppy bulldog jowls and a boxer's bent nose. He greeted us with recognition because we had passed on the river several times over previous days. I have spent enough time in London to recognise his indigenous tones and glottal stops as more born-and-bred than estuarine acquisition. His mannerisms were also familiar. He at first appeared courteous and friendly when asking after our journey. He was, however, more interested in telling us about his own journeys and opinions. Mark gave him a very brief résumé of our trip, but I could see in the glaze of his bloodshot, watery eyes a desperate wish to be 'back to me' as soon as he could interrupt. He called down to his wife below deck intermittently, 'They've ran da-a-n from Cricklade they 'ave, Marge'.

We never saw Marge, and later speculated that there was not actually a Marge down there at all. Diamond Geezer, as we called him, was a part-time rowing official. He told us that he now lived on the river and that he is called upon from time to time to officiate at races. He insisted that he was the best in the business. He rambled on about life on the Thames, the state of the country, and how much better things used to be. Being in white, male company, he felt safe bemoaning immigrant Britain, and offered veiled threats on how he would deal with things, usually ending with either, 'I'll tell you that for nothing', or 'That's not a threat or a promise, it's information'. He did at least tell us about a campsite for us to stay at on our last night. It was at Laleham seven miles away. Mark was quietly squatting on the concrete, giving the unpleasant old chap a good listening to while slowly folding away the tiny kettle stove.

We left a respectable time after paddling away before verbally assassinating the old man's character between us. We might have been completely wrong about him. He had, after all, found his own way to spend his retirement. He was assured in himself and lived independently with pride in his boat. On the other hand, cocky bigots are a menace to society.

At the time of passing, Runnymede – and a chance to visit the field where the Magna Carta was sealed – was not possible because of a foot and mouth disease incident. This Magna Carta, which guaranteed to all free men immunity from illegal imprisonment, is seen as a foundation stone of democracy. The year 1215, for most of us, is just another dull date from school history lessons. The Magna Carta Memorial is at Runnymede, as too is an American memorial to J F Kennedy. Americans are frequent visitors.

The river had very gradually deepened, and the width had become constant. We continued all afternoon through the suburbia which is Staines, exchanging views on what Diamond Geezer was hiding below deck. The river was criss-crossing roads and motorways and weaving among lakes and reservoirs. This is a reminder of how vital the Thames remains as a water source for Londoners. Every day, millions of litres of water are diverted from the Thames into reservoirs to later be cleaned, filtered, and piped into homes.

※

We soon reached Laleham where we found the campsite as recommended. The feeling of the environment was now quite different: the constant background hum of urban life; the smell of the air; the litter here and there – even the demeanour of the staff taking our few quid to camp. There was an imperceptible air of selfishness. Even the grass where we hauled up our boats was seemingly saying, 'You can't park those here, sonny'. We had enjoyed another fine day and we were not going to let grass with attitude spoil the evening.

The final leg of the non-tidal Thames was now a short run to Teddington Lock, thirteen miles away. It would be a long day, because we wanted to leave the boats at Teddington and taxi all the way back to Cricklade, then collect the boats on the way home. We made an early start with more fine weather. The morning passed on a twisting and turning journey, with many more reservoirs and waterworks on all sides. We continued to see kingfishers, and there were also heron stilting in the shallows or flying above with huge broad wings. Mallard and Canada geese were everywhere on the water and gulls were above. Mark spotted a cormorant taking a small eel. Parakeets, a successful escapee species, screamed overhead like flying daggers. The water insects seem to be in greater abundance in these parts than in the more rural areas. It is often said that in London you are never more than a few metres from a rat. We saw rats on the muddy banks around Kingston.

We stopped at Hampton Court Palace where the river front is met with freshly gilded ornate iron gates, bizarrely protected by a more recent iron fence. A clock here still shows the time of high tide at London Bridge. The river connection to London would have been important and frequently in use in past centuries. Hampton Court Palace was the favourite palace of Henry VIII and royal barges would have been a common sight travelling back and forth, with the timing of tide flow key to the speed of travel. Functional river transport outside of the centre of London hardly now exists.

Dave had told Mike, an old university friend who lives nearby, of our impending arrival at Teddington, and he was there at the lock to cheer us to our finishing line.

We had started at 80 metres above sea level and here we were 3.83 metres above sea level. We had been through forty-four locks. Thames Water tells us that the effect of the tide at Teddington, now that the water flowing over the weir is pushed back by the tide twice a day, is such that the water can take anything between three weeks and three months to reach the open sea. The brackish water and ebb and flow of tides from here on lends a quite different character to the river. We would tackle tidal stretches of the Thames another time.

Photo by Mike Tweedale

I had texted a time for my Iranian friend from our first camp to collect us, and he met us as arranged with a huge smile. We emptied the boats and made them as secure as we felt necessary, then we set off in the cab, back up the M4, to reunite with my truck. I caught up on my friend's story a little – on how he had come to be living in a tent. His family had fled Iran because of the revolution overthrowing the Shah in 1977, when he was a young boy, so he felt completely British. He had a sad tale of a wife leaving him with obligations that he could not meet. He had the plans and hopes that keep us going when life is not what we expect. On that car journey back to the Land Rover, all three of us could not keep our eyes or ears in working mode. You never sleep as well as you might with this kind of camping, and we were physically weary. Like mucky active working dogs at the end of a long day, we were all asleep within ten minutes.

CHAPTER 3

THE WYE

A hawk will consider its shadow

The Wye is a river well paddled. The river is said to be the home of the package holiday. In the 1770s, the Reverend John Egerton commissioned a boat to tour the river with a number of guests. William Gilpin helped to popularise the Wye Tour, publishing in 1782 a book with the soundbite title, *Observations on the River Wye: and Several Parts of South Wales, & C. Relative Chiefly to Picturesque Beauty; Made in the Summer of the Year 1770*. With trouble in Europe, the traditional Grand Tour was considered unsafe, so the privileged classes were encouraged to seek out the romantic closer to home.

The Wye has a long-admired landscape as it charges its way through the rugged Welsh hills. Once in England, it meanders, with looping arcs, on its serpentine journey across the plain of Herefordshire and through the canyons at Symonds Yat to the Severn Estuary at Chepstow. It passes, on its way, castles, churches, and magnificent peaceful ruins.

O sylvan Wye! thou wanderer thro' the woods.
How often has my spirit turned to thee!
(Wordsworth)

I would guess that neither Wordsworth nor Gilpin would approve of our hilarity as the three of us crowded around the village sign for a snap where we put in to start our own Wye Tour near Aberllynfi, or the English name, Three Cocks!

We were equipped with Mark's scout double and the brittle fibreglass single *The Sulker*. We had found a spot to leave the vehicle quite close to the water at Glasbury Bridge, and I would return by taxi on completion, when we reached Chepstow a hundred miles downriver.

The water levels were said to be low for early summer and the river here was shallow and fairly rapid. On this first day of our journey, there were to be many small rapids along a gloriously free-flowing section of river, with the Black Mountains always present to the south.

We chatted excitedly as the relief of being away and afloat pumped freedom through our veins. The first few hours of all our expeditions leave me with a

RIVER WYE
9TH-14TH APRIL 2010
100 MILES
THREE CO
EEL
20-mile day
13-mile day
WHITNEY-ON-WYE
HEREFORD
HOARWITHY
PRESTON-ON-WYE
BREADWARDINE
N
E
W
S
HAY-ON-WYE
E
W
HUP!
HUP!
HUP!
HUP!
GLASBURY
START
THREE COCKS
COMFORT!
BIMBLE!
SPEED!!
ZOOM!!
10
20
30
40
MILES

HEY! GET OFFA!
DYKE
Dave Chisholm FRGS
S
NI
I
W
E
F
HOLME LACY
20-mile day
ROSS-ON-WYE
KERNE BRIDGE
23-mile day
SYMONDS YAT
REDBROOK
MOLE!
MONMOUTH
E
W
WHITEBROOK
BROCKWEIR
15-mile day
TINTERN
Abbey
St Catherine's Church
FINISH
CHEPSTOW
9-mile day
CAMP
E ENGLAND
W WALES

strong sense of release. It feels like the beginning of something. It's rejuvenating. The water was clear and rustled like leaves on its broken surface under the grey skies of the day. Dave twisted back in the front of the double where I was at the rear. He cracked an exaggerated smile and pulled down his cap and gave the thumbs-up to Mark, who smiled, ducked his head in salute, and crashed the water with one paddle, as a signal of glee. Here we go again …

Dave made a great fuss about Lord Hereford's Knob, a high point of the northwest scarp of the Black Mountains, as it came into view. Hay Bluff, the other prominent peak, was hardly mentioned. It was cool and breezy. A slight shower spread, like a transparent curtain, folding and shimmering over the open farmland on both sides of the river.

We were soon expecting a little excitement in water conditions at Boatside weir. We approached cautiously, but there were little more than some mildly faster white channels with a clear, faster chute to the right-hand bank. *OK*, I thought, first challenge behind us. My breathing told me that the exercise of our efforts should be to slow down and settle into a regular tempo that we could maintain. 'Calm down. Early days,' I called to the others.

Hay-on-Wye was our first conurbation and the first bridge. The 1950s concrete construction is very high over the river, with little charm, and underneath we encountered shallow rapids. We knew that kayaking was popular all along the Wye, and Mark pointed out evidence of kayak hire and outdoor centre operations at a landing stage after the bridge. Despite its popularity, through the whole trip, perhaps because it was out of season, we didn't see any other kayaks.

We discussed a possible stop-off in the town, known for its second-hand books and literary festival, but it seemed too soon, and so we pressed on through open farmland. We stopped to make tea on a shingle promontory opposite the receding bank of a sinuous meander.

Dave and I pulled our boat clear of the water and set up the kettle. Mark pulled up the single and dug out the tea from a dry bag.

We sat together on a whitewashed log and watched the mouse-grey mudbank in front of us. Mark had settled on one end of the log, but when I joined Dave at the other end, Mark was catapulted off his perch, spilling his tea. Dave laughed openly as Mark shook his head with a one-sided smile. Mark has a way of looking at you that seems to be saying, 'OK, fair cop', as he hunches his shoulders and puffs air into his lips. I lit the small stove to refill Mark's mug.

The bank was 2 or 3 metres in height with scores of round holes, shot through in a random fashion. Sand martins flitted and dived acrobatically, and continually, around these nest burrows. The earthy scent of the water and mud blew around in the breeze. A stand of alder trees behind us, their bright young leaves only just beyond budding, bent towards the water and shimmered stiffly. We were feeling light and glad to be out together. Our early error was that we'd run out of tea bags already.

In the Quartermaster's Stores

Dave is charged with general supplies and this is his account of that responsibility:

I'm not bad at maps and journey planning, but Mark is better, and Nick more interested. So it made sense for me to fill the vacant quartermaster role.

The limiting factors when choosing supplies are size and weight. Light compact food, which is easy to cook, is filling, provides lots of energy and is also tasty, is best. Planning and resupply are important: it's not only armies that march on their stomachs!

The big blue dry bag is stowed deep in my boat. By the end of any trip, it resembles a dustbin more than a food store. It contains tins (e.g. baked beans and tomatoes), pesto, tomato puree, pasta, cereal (Shredded Wheat is good), bacon, cheese, garlic, onions, salami, mixed herbs, chilli or Tabasco, tea, and instant soup.

Delicates, like milk, eggs, bread, fruit and salad, tend to be crammed near the top, in small remaining spaces once everything else has been packed away.

The popular snack bag is in my cockpit, within easy reach while paddling. We exert ourselves, so lucky dips at rest breaks for mixed nuts, biscuits, sweets, chocolate or cereal bars are vital to keep spirits up and energy flowing.

Frequent attention is required as there is not enough space for all these items at any one time. We need to stay aware of what we have, how long it will last, and when resupply will be possible.

Readers will notice that we do have a few luxuries. River Ratting is, after all, more holiday than expedition. Beer is no good for the mobile bar: it's too voluminous. Spirits are best. Usually whisky for Nick and me, and rum for Mark. The occasional bottle of wine slips through security, and, 'when in Rome …' comes into play. So, for example, powerful raki was on board in Albania.

Plenty of water is needed and the big concertina carrier is always difficult to stow away. It refills our carabiner-clipped water bottles, and is needed for cooking too.

Mark carries a small amount of cooking oil in his brilliantly conceived portable riverbank cooker and kitchen set. It includes a Trangia set, gas, light-

weight utensils, cutting mat, scourer, washing-up liquid and other essentials. This is only trumped by his 'trowel set', which is stored at a safe distance, and is speedily accessible when a River Rat has 'a mole at the counter'!

Quartermastering should be an invisible job, but if not done properly, everyone knows! Yet, after a hard day on the water, when we enjoy a warm glow from food and drink and the day's Ratting is mulled over, it can be most satisfying.

A fun tale to finish with. We tend not to be salad dodgers, but Mark carried a lettuce, 'trussed up' in his foredeck netting, that somehow managed to outlast our Scotland journey. It was 2014. An omen perhaps of Britain's political disasters that were beginning to unfold.

※

The rain held off from weighty clouds as we paddled the afternoon away. The valley had been imperceptibly widening and the water deepening throughout the day. The bridge at Whitney was the next landmark. The bridge is a distinctive construction, with three central spans of timber with stone arches to either side. It is also unusual because it is a privately owned toll bridge. The bridge is immediately followed by a series of ruffly rapids that came and went to speed us effortlessly for the next couple of miles.

We decided to set up camp by late afternoon and found a suitable spot on the riverbank near a corrugated iron fisherman's hut. Nearby is the spot where, in 1927, in the heyday of salmon fishing on the Wye, the largest rod-caught salmon ever landed in Britain was hauled out of the water, weighing in at a giant sixty pounds. The catcher, one Doreen Davey, is said to have received at least one marriage proposal as a result of her success. I pointed this out to the boys. Dave lifted his thick black eyebrows and let out a long slow whistle. Mark raised the back of his wrist to his forehead and looked to the sky.

There are still a few ghillies remaining on the river where once there were scores. The salmon catches this century are much diminished in numbers and fish size. In the twentieth century it was de rigueur for the great and the good to be seen salmon fishing on the Wye. This included royalty from Britain and around the world, prime ministers, and celebrities. The idea that a ghillie, or gillie, is a servant in attendance to his male master, is also, thankfully, diminished. The expertise of these individuals is remarkable.

It had been a long day with a dawn start and a five-hour car journey before launching. We made it easy on ourselves and wandered uphill to the north and The Sun Inn at Winforton for supper and a debrief. It had become chilly, so the warmth of the indoors was welcome. My home in Kent is known for its orchards, and Hereford has a similar fame, especially for cider apples. Local cider was on offer. I would love to enjoy cider. I tried my best to enjoy it when I lived in Bristol, where it has a long tradition. I've tried to drink it in Asturias, in northern Spain, where it is a way of life and they pour it from a great height to oxidise the liquid. I just don't like it. I made a poor and embarrassing effort to remember The Wurzels' lyrics while the boys tried kindly to hide their embarrassment.

We made our way gingerly back in the dark. Mark and I settled into our small tent, leaving Dave a snore's distance away in his bivvy behind the shed.

The first night always proves a bit stiff on the muscles, so, as we staggered out in the morning, we moved awkwardly like puppets until the bodies' natural joint lubricant began to ease the creaks. Dave heroically made an early call into the village for tea bags. There was no shop, so he simply knocked on the first door and a pleasant middle-aged woman offered him as many as he wanted. The kindness of strangers is a wonderful thing. We've asked for help, one way or another, on all our river trips, and it is very unusual to be disappointed. The stranger the stranger, the more life-affirming and gratifying an experience the received help becomes.

The first mile of the day was bright sunshine. We were quickly met by some glittering easy rapids that focused our concentration for a few minutes. Following on was gentle and meandering with an ever-widening valley. Mark had seen an oxbow lake on the map. This is his account:

From a kayaker's viewpoint, it's not easy to know where you are. Bridges become a welcome sight because they pinpoint your position. Oxbow lakes are a feature that we all learn about in geography lessons, but rarely do we see one and recognise what it is, so I was keen to track it down. We located what appeared to be the correct bend in the river, tied up, and set off walking across the field, looking for a hidden lake nearby. The damp meadow was filled with cuckoo flowers in bloom. We had been looking one bend too soon. We found the lake a further hundred metres downriver. It was obvious where the two ends would have joined the river, its parent, before it went alone.

The flowers, the water, and the many shades of shimmering green to the weeds of the lake and grass in the meadow lent the scene the look of a Pre-Raphaelite painting. On the edge of the lake was a huge and ancient sycamore. Although only naturalised in Britain for six hundred years, the sycamore, and its distinctive helicopter seeds, has gained a place of affection. All things change and evolve and this old tree was nearing its end. The inside was completely hollow, with a split the full height of its trunk on one side. It was impossible to resist climbing in. I wasn't sure if I felt more like a bear or a blue tit. The lower limbs of the old tree had sagged to the ground, and were now helping support its declining years. Mark was up these and above my head in a few seconds. Dave was sizing up the lake for a swim. 'Get that monkey in the boat,' shouted Dave. We decided to press on.

Bredwardine Bridge was soon in front of us. The brick bridge has six arches. At this water level, with reflection in the flat water, the appearance was of six perfect circles, through which we would glide. Near the previous night's fishing-hut stop, we had seen a white marker indicating the unbelievable water height that occurred in the 1795 flood. This bridge, built in 1769, was the first bridge to survive that disaster. All bridges downriver from here were destroyed. Like most old bridges it had once been a toll bridge. What exists now is in fact a rebuild from 1922. The exact details were faithfully reproduced. You wouldn't know. Even the bricks look to be original.

The distinctive earthen remains of a motte-and-bailey castle were on our right. The character of the banks became more wooded, with greenery overhanging the water at all times. We quietly paddled for a few sinuous, muted miles before the sudden appearance of cliffs on the left bank that looked like they were worn away from a vast heap of ferrous oxide. The crumbling pink-red sandstone banks, 50 metres above us, known as 'The Scar', were crowned with old beech trees. The roots, clawing hopefully into rock and soil, were undermined and visible like knuckled fists clinging on desperately. Under the shade of the cliffs, in the shallow water we could see a large shoal of substantially sized chub.

We then passed a strange craft with four paddling occupants, one on each corner, three men and one woman. It was a bit like a homemade catamaran, tied together with blue nylon rope. We briefly chatted to the paddlers, a charity team in practice for a raft race. People will find all manner of ways to make things more difficult. They were good-humoured, tired, and determined to have fun.

The escarpment soon gave way to farmland and orchards. Progress was easy. The sun threw glinting sparks and shards all around us. It was still and quiet. Mark started to sing. 'Go ahead and sound happy,' commented Dave, 'everything living nearby has scarpered'.

We knew that Monnington Falls was nearby and that it could be tricky. We needed to approach with caution. There was once a weir at this point. Long demolished, there still remain angled bedrock reefs that may or may not be submerged, depending on water levels. The current was adequately mild to allow us inspection as we approached. There was a distinct hazard on the left rapid channel: a tree had lodged between rocks. We needed to avoid this. The concentration kept trepidation at bay. We were safe enough threading our way between only partially submerged rocks to the right side. Waves lapped, scooping generously immediately after the rocks, and Mark, in *The Sulker*, with only his rudimentary spray deck, took on board a fair bit of water.

We eventually pulled up to empty Mark's boat opposite Weir Garden, some distance further on. With its formal structure and terraced walls, this was a complete change in character to the waterfront. We sat for a while, on damp grass, under a magnificent weeping willow that cascaded in bright new leaf into the river below. Hereford was only a short paddle away, where we would spend our second night.

Approaching the only city on the Wye, there are some private houses on the banks, and a disused rail bridge, now a footbridge, then Hereford Rowing Club, and a modern road bridge. Further down river, there is the very beautiful, fifteenth-century Wye Bridge, with the pinnacles and castellations of Hereford Cathedral behind. The stone is, like The Scar upriver, a warm, dusky pink-red colour. We decided to backtrack a little and returned to the rowing club where, for a small fee, you can pitch up.

We secured our boats, then Mark and I put the tent up alongside our boats on a small paddock next to the club's main building. The club has been here since 1859 and has won a string of successes. The current club building, built in 1958, functions well, but has a dreary institutional appearance.

Hereford is a small, attractive cathedral city, characterised by both black-and-white buildings and extensive use of local red sandstone. We spent the early evening walking through the streets and eating chips. The drizzly rain was turning the cathedral stone a dark shade. The light was dimming. We returned to the rowing club where we had use of a shower, pulled on dry clothes and found the club bar open and hosting a wedding reception.

We sat ourselves among the shiny Moss Bros. suits of the wedding party. There were dolled-up young women with equally shiny hair, and testosterone-charged young men buzzing around them. There were small children dressed like adults, and balloons and streamers, mums and dads trying to impress each other, and the happy young couple. It was assumed that we were guests, and by the end of the evening, we thought we were more or less family. It didn't seem like that in the morning as we tried to recall whom we had offended.

It took us forty minutes of early morning paddling to see the back of Hereford, and after a few kilometres of raised bank to our left, we were at the confluence of the Lugg. From here to Capler Camp, six miles or so downriver, on the east bank, there is a notable geological feature called the Woolhope Dome. This is a range of beautiful rolling hills of woods and wild flower meadows. It is the soft Silurian limestones and sandstones, the bedrock of these hills, spreading over millennia as river alluvium, that gives the whole area its distinctive rusty looking soil character.

We paddled peacefully under blue skies heavy with broken cumulus cloud marching along with us above, and sinuous weed with darting fry in constant movement below. The larger fish faced into the current, expending just enough energy to tread water. They seemed to tolerate our passage stoically.

We had scooted on through bumpy rapids as we picked our way past a series of long thin islands, when we found ourselves approaching the strange sight of five huge stone columns, three of which were rising from the water. They appeared like Brâncuşi's 'Endless Column', or a monolithic Antony Gormley sculpture. They seemed like sacred protectors of the river. Mark is an expert mountaineer and a top-level alpinist. He has scaled the Eiger, the Matterhorn and Mont Blanc. He has also recently climbed the Old Man of Hoy, a forbidding giant sea stack, lashed by North Atlantic winds. He was weighing up the possibility of scaling these tottering towers. What remains here are the stone relics of Bellingham Bridge, a dismantled railway viaduct. We stopped paddling and let the current take us quietly through, as if reverence was demanded.

We tend to change places quite frequently so that we all share being in the single, at the front, or at the back, of the double kayak. We've never squabbled about this in all our trips and the three of us live an easy existence as we make progress along our journeys. Stopping points seem to come by invisible consensus. It had become time for a change. After the plain-looking Hoarwithy Bridge, with its strange-looking former toll house, more like a small tower with irregularly spaced small windows and steep slate roof structure, we pulled up on a shingle bank. We had covered plenty of distance, it was warm, we were more or less dry, so we decided to walk into the village for a peruse and for some food.

We didn't know that St Catherine's church was a well-known eccentricity, but as we approached, it was obvious that it was something unusual. It looks like a folly and has an Italianate feeling, with its rising square section tower and Romanesque-looking windows that survey the village and countryside. The church was built between 1870 and 1900 on the whim of Prebendary William Poole, to the design of John Pollard Seddon. We walked through a Romanesque cloister, the afternoon sun streaming through each round arch, highlighted by dust swirling in a paisley pattern, as our wet, inappropriate clothes still dripped onto the cool flagstone floor. Inside we remained hushed. The interior is rich in colour and atmosphere. There are marble columns and the altar is decorated with a tiger's eye cross, enhanced with inlaid lapis lazuli, above which gleams a golden mosaic in a half dome, with a Byzantine-looking Christ figure. There is elaborate carving, copies of Venetian oil lamps, and the vibrant stained-glass windows allow striking colour to pervade throughout with rainbow intensity. One of the windows on the west wall, an ethereal blue angel figure with red wings and a golden yellow trumpet, is by Edward Coley Burne-Jones. Hereford Cathedral is home to the *Mappa Mundi*, and a copy was hanging between monuments to locals fallen in the wars. 'Map of the world,' I said, to immediate derision from Dave commenting on my habit of stating the obvious.

There were also children's paintings and Easter displays of Calvary scenes that were inevitably gaudy and crude, made of silver paper and tatty snippets of cloth. The contrast with the refined architectural detail made them seem at once appealing and sentimental but also desperate and, like our clothing, was like fly-tipping in the splendour of the church.

We found a pub for a good meal and were once again interrupting a family occasion. Here late-afternoon inebriation after a christening was competing with TV football in the next-door bar. Half the family was intent on watching whatever big game was in progress and slipped repeatedly in and out of the reception to the other bar, where we were ensconced, while the other half of the family let them believe scornfully that they didn't know what was going on.

Back on the water, the remaining afternoon was slow and warm. Conditions allowed us to talk across the water easily to each other. The landscape was fresh and super green. We pulled up for the day after reaching a wonderful suspension footbridge that elegantly strung itself over the river. As we drifted underneath, we could hear the evening breeze through the steels like a whispering Welsh harp, reminding us that this has not forever been England. The village of Sellack was on one side of the river and the spire of St Tysilio's Church, just above what looked like a flood plain, stood perpendicular on the opposite bank.

We had settled into a camp routine by now and it felt comfortable watching Dave and Mark that evening move about slowly as they carried out the various tasks needed to bed down. Once a camp has been established for the evening, the immediate features become peculiarly comfortable. You know which log is where, you know how to move around the terrain, each rock or hummock becomes familiar remarkably quickly. You've set your bed up. It becomes home. We sat around our tiny fire, discussing the following day's plans, with pullovers slung over shoulders to keep the outer chill off our huddle, while inside our cosy circle was a glow of warm flickering colour, warm food, and warm chat.

Travelling by any kind of canoe is special. Travel by car, or any mechanical transport, by comparison is mean and ignoble. In a canoe you travel with joy. The cleansing beat of nature resounds through your body and you progress by your physical efforts. You are light and the stagnations of life become fluid, like blood returning to numbed limbs. The mundane becomes wondrous and the wondrous becomes celestial. Time on the river isn't like normal time, it is slow and stretched. Problems elsewhere can be put aside.

Our next day's journey would take us an easy 23 miles through delightful scenic topography to Symonds Yat.

Everyone has a different morning demeanour. I'm a good early riser and I know the boys enjoy my early kettle habit. Dave is slow in the mornings, climbing out of his bivvy bag like a bear out of hibernation. His thick stiff white hair never out of place, he stretches carefully and often hobbles out of site early with the trowel. Mark is usually second up and he seems to wake in two stages. First, he sits or stands, after which he stays still for a minute or so, then he seems to go straight into normal function.

While setting up for morning tea, I watched a sparrowhawk for ten minutes. They are rewarding hunters to watch. This was a large-looking hawk, so was probably a female. It had perched on an oak tree a hundred metres away, and I had watched it try to ambush a small bird on the hedgerow near our camp, failing, and returning to the same perch. They have short, broad wings adapted to lunatic speeds, hunting with deft manoeuvres among trees. The hawk will consider its shadow when hunting and use stealth and cunning, using buildings and trees for cover and surprise. A second dash ended in a burst of feathers and I saw her returning with quarry hanging from her undercarriage.

Early in the morning, once underway, we noticed, raised among a jumble of flotsam, a swan on its nest, its head nestled back among its wings. There is a building-site feel to a swan's nest. This one was about 2 metres across at the base and had been stacked and woven on sloping ground, so the construction had to intelligently produce a level plateau for the large birds. The sitting bird's mate billowed past us like an elegant clipper, hissing menacingly.

The river soon took a huge loop from eastward to westward, with the characteristic escarpment on the turn. The still air was alive with insects and the sound of reed buntings, blackcap, and warblers was a constant pleasure. A mallard with her brood of fluffy ping-pong-ball-sized chicks paraded close to the water's edge, paddling between the white flowers of water-crowfoot that swayed with the current. Another suspension footbridge spanned the river. This is Foy Bridge. It seems to be miniature and is of steel construction. It has elegant finials on the two supporting towers that themselves are of Meccano-like construction. The walkway is timber slats. The structure is in a state of mild and pleasant decay. Some gentle rust stains decorate the surface with a soft orange patination, which is echoed in the arsenic-coloured lichen that covers much of the paintwork, which is peeling and cracking like old skin. The spans emerge from the willowy banks with the yellow punctuation of lesser celandine beneath. The access paths to the bridge point to the fact that it is well used, and fishing here is popular. Buildings and structures generally require maintenance, repair and repainting, but there is a period of grace before this becomes essential, during which they acquire the charm and appeal that comes with age and use. In that regard, at the time that we floated under its criss-cross balustrade, Foy Bridge was in its prime.

The banks were becoming thinly wooded, on steep slopes, unmanaged, rarely visited, and they presented an untidy, natural landscape of fallen trees in all stages of decomposition, with other trees upright and vigorous. The spring leaf growth was not yet obscuring the red soil, detritus, and scrappy brambles of the woodland floor. The wooded borders were interspersed with flat areas, where pasture or crops spread flat into the distance. The livestock was sheep and cattle.

Later that morning we paddled up close to a magnificent Hereford bull that was hock-deep in the water, surrounded by his harem of russet and alluring heifers with shining silky coats. There are few animals that display a musculature of such power. Our large friend here eyed us lethargically and was as calm as our own flotilla that surveyed him in silence. Hereford cattle are now a popular breed in over fifty countries. I tried to tell Dave and Mark about the Uruguayan town of Frey Bentos, a name that has a long association with Herefords but which most of us don't know is a place, thinking simply it is a tinned pie. I was yawned out.

There was another strange bridge ruin, presenting the same abandoned stone pillars that we had seen upriver. This was the former Backney Bridge. The river now plunges due south and we were then in sight of the silhouette of Ross-on-Wye. We pulled our boats onto the steps of the rowing club and spent time in the town stocking up with supplies. We needed another gas canister. We didn't miss the chance to scoff down a fried breakfast for lunch. The town is like a smaller version of Hereford, with both black-and-white ancient timber and weathered sandstone buildings. The town has a long history of Outward Bound tourism that seems both modern and school-orientated, as well as long-established and Victorian. The river is central to this role and we were playing our part in that tradition.

Onwards from Ross, we encountered some wind that scattered frothy white crests across the water's surface. Goodrich Castle rose above the treeline on our right. The castle is in the perfect state of ruination for it to have been an essential stop for those on the Wye Tour. The countryside became increasingly rugged and we were whisked along on small but persistent rapids at regular intervals. The familiar meandering continued, but the current was becoming stronger and the river began to feel more substantial and mature. The wooded embankments became steeper. The agricultural elements disappeared as a wilder nature began to dominate. We were soon under Kerne Bridge, the location of a pre-Roman ford, now a stone bridge of five arches. Dave pointed out the rope marks, gouged and worn into the pillars from the manual hauling of barges through the years. We were caught out immediately after the bridge by some lumpy rapids that both kayaks took at the roughest section, which focused all our minds for a few minutes. This bridge marks the northern end of the Upper Wye Gorge. Sand martins were here in great numbers, darting and swooping at dare-devil speed, close to the water, in a continual search for insect protein. Their nest holes pockmarked the muddy banks. By the time we had reached Yat Rock, we were within the Forest of Dean. The environment had now become majestic, and the romantic drama of the Wye, vaunted by past poets and artists, was truly around us.

I had been in *The Sulker* most of the afternoon, and the rapids had left my vessel with a lot of water swilling around my legs and seat. I was beginning to feel cold, so I was relieved to pack up paddling for the day, and we pulled up as soon as we found a secluded spot. We dried off and brewed tea. Mark discussed the route he had planned to take us up to the top of Yat Rock.

The steep walk after the exertions of the day was arduous, but none of us was going to admit that. Dave strode on strongly and told us about *Offa's Dyke Walking Holidays* that he and his wife, Josie, had set up before the arrival of their three children. We were now walking a section of the Dyke. Mark has smaller, quicker paces, and his light Norfolk lilt lifts up and down as we chat, as easily as his tirelessly fit frame. The bluebells and anemones accompanied us through the woodland. Rocky outcrops protruded here and there. At a flat and damper part of the terrain, we were overwhelmed by the heady scent of wild garlic, just now in flower. We were travelling from the river due west and upwards, towards the view of the river a few miles upstream, across the pinch point of a looping meander.

Once at the top, the view was awe inspiring and far reaching. A light mist took the focus off the junctions where the grey-white cliffs were overtaken by an assortment of vegetation and thick ropes of flaking honeysuckle vines, as if the oatmeal colours had been softened together with an air brush. Raptors soared above, below and in front of us. Behind us, a nuthatch scaled the riven bark of an old oak stunted from the wind and exposure. An official RSPB telescope and guide was stationed here. The guide was youngish and enthusiastic. He trained the telescope onto a peregrine that was perched below and north, on a rock ledge some one hundred metres away.

The peregrine is the top gun of the avian world. The fastest living animal of any sort. J A Baker's *The Peregrine* is a wonderful account of that individual's obsession with this bird. When he sat down to condense many years of notes into a poetic diary, closely observing the falcon's behaviour in every visceral detail, he thought that he was recording a vanishing world. The widespread use of the pesticide DDT at this time – the late 1960s – had started to decimate the UK population of raptors, and the Essex side of the Thames Estuary, where Baker followed his obsession day by day, was becoming an ever-more urban environment. There are only a few pockets of success in the depressing story of the twenty-first century's rapidly declining diversity and health of nature, but the peregrine population is one of them, as it has recovered and thrived in the Thames Estuary since that time. The peregrine that we were studying stood unmoved and watchful, and, like us, faced into the breeze, observing its rugged territory. Mark sat next to the guide and took off his hat, his mousy hair softly flopping as he nodded his head emphatically at the guide's comments. Dave and I leant out over the ledge, enjoying the dizzying view below.

We extended our walking that evening with a trek to find beer and ready-made food at The Saracens Head. They are used to canoeists and walkers, so our weathered appearance didn't frighten the staff. We use the toilet hand driers to warm and dry more than our hands when we have the opportunity, so we returned to our boats cheerful and dry that night.

The morning quickly saw us arriving at Symonds Yat rapid. We had decided to negotiate the challenge on an ad hoc basis, without a stop to view. We could see lively bars of white water ahead on the left side of a small island. The right-hand side looked too narrow, but generally, Dave and I in the double, were following Mark's path in *The Sulker*. The rapids are often used as an early training ground for white-water kayaking and the current is accelerated by man-made groynes on either bank. The rapids only last for a brief 150 metres and we had no trouble steering a straight course through them.

The current quickly slowed to a stately pace and the wooded banks on both sides were thick and vibrant, more so than the wooded borders upstream that were scraggy in character with more conifers. Craggy limestone was visible through and above the canopy as we approached an area on the left bank known menacingly as 'The Slaughter', thought to be the location of a bloody confrontation between the Ancient Britons and the Roman invaders. The river here is the Welsh–English border and Dave said he was looking forward to the upcoming slaughter he was hoping for when the two nations were to meet on the rugby pitch that weekend.

Easy, shallow rapids follow for a fair distance. We tried to progress together, side by side, letting the current take us and simply direct our kayaks in a straight line. We were able to chat and discuss what was ahead and when to stop for a brew. We passed under a swinging footbridge and Lady Park Wood was soon on the left bank. This is an area of great importance to the study of our native woodland as it has been an early rewilding experiment and has been left alone, unmanaged since the last war. The river sways its way through a thick, varied canopy of beech, ash, lime, oak, and yew. Below the high canopy we could also see holly, hazel and dogwood with spindle and honeysuckle closer still to the woodland floor.

The Seven Sisters Rocks appeared as we followed the bend left. We couldn't count seven. This is an area of extensive and very long-standing limestone quarrying, and high up on the escarpment is King Arthur's Cave. The cave has revealed mammoth and woolly rhinoceros' bones from the last ice age, but more recently, a nineteenth-century character lived here, a fur trapper named Slippery Jim, who, we are told, liked to brag that he hadn't washed for thirty years.

We paddled quietly together and followed the deeper course to the right of Haddock Island. This is the end of the gorge. The river remains running, however, through hills on either side. We pulled up next to the twelfth-century St Peter's Church on our right and hauled the boats onto a grassy field as the late morning sunshine began to warm us all.

※

We pulled off our spray skirts and wandered over to the church for a welcome leg stretch. The limestone church is rendered and painted, which that day appeared as dazzling white. The building is only twenty paces from the river and only 3 or 4 metres from current water levels. Flooding with spring tides must be a problem.

We had seen several flood depth markers along our journey and the marker in this church entrance, dated January 1607, is 2 metres above the church floor. This refers to the greatest natural disaster to occur in recorded British history, when at least two thousand people were killed by a storm surge in the Bristol Channel. It was described at the time as a seven-yard wall of water moving 'faster than a greyhound can run'. A recent book by Mike Hall, *The Severn Tsunami? The Story of Britain's Greatest Natural Disaster*, speculates that it may have been caused by an earthquake below the seabed and he explains that sea defences traditionally maintained by the church had lapsed after Henry VIII had dissolved the monasteries seventy years earlier. He suggests that in any event, a combination of high tides and severe storms would produce such an event every five hundred years.

We were quite close to Monmouth, so we missed out on tea, clambered into our vessels and paddled on to the rowing club with the familiar steps down to the river, where we could safely leave everything and walk to an early lunch destination. The town is in border country and has plenty of confrontational history. I was at university in Wales and both Dave and Mark have spent considerable time in the country too. We discussed the feeling that we all shared, as Englishmen, that there is a mild undercurrent of resentment towards us. This coloured our feelings of the atmosphere that we may have imposed ourselves on the town. The evolving architecture through the centuries has a toy-town appearance. There are small streets with narrow alleys. The gentrification by the 'good life' seekers from more metropolitan places is showing in the artisanal cheese counters and craft ale displays around the town. We found an outside café table to settle and plan the rest of the day. We decided to end our penultimate day at Brockweir, a further 9 miles downriver, and where the Wye becomes tidal. We set off again, a little stiff from the rest and full of tea and bacon.

The river loses its looping meanders on this stretch and it makes a straightening dash south over series after series of mild rapids that speed our journey. We pass the confluence of the Monnow and the Trothy, and two former rail bridges, one of which has lost its span across the river and leads up to the crossing with twenty arches of slightly increasing height, then stops abruptly, like a failed jump attempt. The Forest of Dean proper lies to our east. The rapids near Redbrook are created by huge, smooth boulders that span the river and here we were lucky to see a goosander carrying a brood of her chicks on her back. They have great looks, slightly comical, with a bright red bill, slightly hooked at the end, a distinctive rust-coloured head, with a punk's Mohican at rear. It has the telltale low-water line of the diver on its silvery sleek body. There were heron and moorhens and the daydreamy background of skylarks overhead. We heard the first of the year's swifts screeching like devils, and later in the afternoon, we watched a hobby, which, too, will have just arrived from far away, cruising at low level in front of us, chasing down dragonflies. (The Latin scientific name for the hobby is Falco Subbuteo, and the name was hijacked by the inventor of the board game, Peter Adolph, when he failed to obtain a trademark on his preferred name, Hobby. I'm not sure that anyone plays Subbuteo anymore.)

The river and the breeze had calmed by the time we reached Bigsweir Bridge. The structure is an elegant iron creation from 1828 and the shallow curve of the span above, reflected in the still water below, gave the impression that we were entering the mouth of a giant barbel, with adjacent reeds like the whiskery tendrils of the beast. The symbolism of this is marked by this point being the Normal Tide Limit (NTL), with the consequent changes in ecology, current and water levels.

Offa's Dyke Path follows the riverbank left and the remaining afternoon on the water was a gentle wind down to Brockweir Bridge, an ungraceful steel structure with four simple tubular piers and a flat, latticework-lined span. There was some remaining evidence of the old quayside before we passed under the bridge. We soon found a suitable bank to pull up on and we set about making camp. Dave walked to a farmhouse nearby to ask if they were OK with us resting up for the night on their field. Dave told us that he'd been greeted by a middle-aged woman, and she was not at all happy about his request. She also pointed out that an official campsite was nearby. I've seen, on many occasions, people struggling to say 'no' to Dave when he softens his voice and claims innocence with a chuckling smile, so he won our pitch.

It's difficult to imagine now, but the tree-filled rural village of Brockweir was once an industrial hub, with shipbuilding and factories from the very beginning of the Industrial Revolution. The small port was as far upriver as the larger vessels could travel. The tiny conglomeration of houses, which now has the rustic downhill tumble of a hotchpotch Cornish fishing village, had a wild reputation and once buzzed with the activities of cockfighting, gambling, and prostitution. The Moravian Brethren established a church here to save these sinful souls in 1833.

We made the walk into Brockweir village and found the church door open. The cool interior immediately threw a musty scent about, which combined with beeswax and the smell of old books. The building is a pleasingly simple design with pine pews, white walls and ceilings, and a plain organ on a balcony above the entrance.

Back with our kayaks, we busied ourselves with drying and packing. A fire was not a good idea, as we were not completely welcome at this spot, so we gathered coats and valuables and walked off back towards the village. The workmanlike muddy farmyard had old timber barns as well as open steel structures stacked with hay under barrel-vaulted wriggly tin roofs. A huge green double-decker bus slept happily, tucked into a corner, and looked like it had been parked there for many years. Probably dead, not sleeping, it had cracked flat tyres and peeling mossy paintwork.

We wandered towards the collection of houses and soon heard voices. There were double doors at the end of a recess between two buildings where we could hear some activity. I knocked, then opened the door to a large open hall. There were several table tennis tables erected and in use. The chat stopped and a company of ten or twelve men and women, looking like they were in their seventies and eighties, stood looking at us enquiringly. Our interruption was sudden enough to catch them with their smiles and interactions frozen. One old gent, dapper in an olive-coloured waistcoat and thick white hair, swatting his bat in an open gesture, welcomed us warmly in an accent last heard on the BBC in 1960. He asked how they could help. These were happy people. A pervading warmth exuded from the group like old friends. I wanted to join in. Dave asked where we could find a drink, and they sent us on our way, just around a corner.

The pub was empty but for a rotund landlord and what we took to be the usual know-all permanent drinker in his regular chair at a corner of the bar. The walls were decorated with black-and-white images of old river life, especially the elver fisherman, whose trade here was once thriving. The eel population has suffered a massive reduction in the last thirty years for reasons not fully understood. They were once so plentiful that excess catches of elvers on the Wye were spread on the fields as fertiliser. There is some optimism, however, with recent recorded increases in numbers on the Severn and the Wye. Elvers, known as glass eels, still realise a high price at market. And fishing, both legal and illegal, continues. Like bird migration, fish too share this wonder. With the sudden and sad reduction in European eel population, it has become a much-studied phenomenon and it seems that it has now been firmly established that eels derive positional information from the earth's magnetic field. The thread-like eels start their life near Bermuda in the Sargasso Sea, and drift for two years on the Gulf Stream to European rivers. They change shape on this journey, and once in fresh water, they begin to pigment and swim upstream to thrive – they will be known at this life stage as yellow eels – where they remain for between five and twenty years. In their final life stage, the journey back to the Sargasso, where they spawn and die, they are known as silver eels. This sees them undergoing a remarkable metamorphosis, where their colour changes, their pectoral fins widen, their digestive tract shuts down and their eyes grow to ten times their original size. All this will assist in the final epic journey of their life. A creature with such rounded nobility of purpose in life deserves what protection we can offer.

We huddled around our little table and shared stories, sometimes like secrets with hushed tones, at times with indignation, then emphatically with hand gestures and loud laughter. Mark's gentle voice, when recounting absurdly dangerous crossings of crevasses on glaciers in the alps, or a slip when halfway up some sea stack in Scotland, belies his steely confidence. Dave has a way of jutting his chin forward and raising his large dark eyebrows when emphasising a point. He has a great sense of timing to enhance some insane tale of bobsleigh driving, or a dramatic incident when leading a jungle expedition. The landlord was a kindly chap and tried to take part. The pub bore at the bar, round-faced with taut ruddy skin and greying gingery remnants of hair, warned us not to kayak any further. 'Acres of mud and ambiguous fast currents,' he told us. Well fed and watered, we left with heartfelt good wishes from our landlord, who told us that we had lightened his day, and brought him back to his younger days – which was a little odd, as I think we were older than him.

Walking back along the tree-lined river, now on the darker side of dusk, we were startled by a sprayed plopping splash as a large salmon flopped back into the water. This put us on alert. We saw, at house height, a shuddering movement over the ink-black rippled river. The vision from a side glance came and went again and again. I couldn't be sure. Squinting hard, the apparition became apparent. It appeared and disappeared from places unexpected like a diving duck. The twitching crazy zig-zag bumph, darting here and there in random silence could have been a falling leaf. His leathery cocktail umbrella wings flickered like an old movie in the soft cool air. Insects flashed with moonlit highlights, like flashing bombs of damaged celluloid. We lost sight of him again. An uneasy quiet blackness followed. He suddenly came back flapping close, and mild panic welled in my throat. I saw the others stooping fast, their eyes wide white. The moist air sparked with the fuzz of electrostatic tension. He batted off, agile like a pinball between branches. This was a long-eared bat, and as he crossed the moon, I could fleetingly see light through his large veined ears. He seemed vulnerable, fragile. We made our way back along the riverbank to our night's rest, moving slowly, muttering gently.

Gleaming sun greeted us on the morning of our last day on the river. We were afloat early because we needed to time the tides correctly and have the tide with us for most of the paddle – and to arrive at Chepstow when the tide was close to high. If we had the timing wrong, the outcome could be dangerous. The Wye at Chepstow has among the greatest tidal variation in the entire world. All within 50 metres of the riverbank, from its lowest point, the tide rises 13.4 metres within four hours.

The morning mist still hung on the river, rose tinted and lying in soft folds between woods and architecture. This gave us an ethereal view of the ruined Tintern Abbey as we rounded the first sharp bend of the day, with the perpendicular skeleton reaching to a backdrop of candy floss pink sky. The abbey must have been the romantic ecclesiastical ruin par excellence for those early tourists. Turner, Wordsworth and countless other artists and writers have admired this view.

The river became increasingly yellow and opaque. Branches and all manner of detritus floated alongside us, slipping in and out of view, partially submerged, bobbing and racing on. The red earth and rocks from upriver had disappeared. This final eight or nine miles was quite different. Mud lined the banks, slippery and silver like the back of an eel. For most of the morning, the banks rose steeply and we were overshadowed by shoulders of soaring limestone cliffs through what is Wye's lower gorge. To our left, shortly after Tintern was the Devil's Pulpit, a high-level geological quirk where a flat-topped rock has formed, jutting out from the cliff. This is a well-known scenic viewpoint and another favourite of the Wye Tour. Further on is the Black Cliff. 'Good rock, unpolished. Mainly bolted climbing,' commented Mark.

Several looping bends followed as the river widened. Dave and I were in the double. As we slowly rounded on the outer side of a bend, we were caught in a strange side current that was trying to turn the boat. The tide was now fully pushing seaward and the sense of heavy water pressing the gunwale was alarming. We had read that this stretch was strictly for experienced kayakers and this was one of our earlier journeys. We were unsure. I thought of the miserable local from the previous night. I could see Dave's body tensing. 'Gently left,' I said, steering us safely straight.

'OK, boys?' shouted Mark from behind. All was well.

The aura and scent of the now brackish water felt like new territory. The first tang of salt was unmistakable. Grey was taking over all around for some time. The sun had disappeared, and it was grey overhead. The grey mud led up to grey cliffs and the sinewy grey ropes of old man's beard tumbled down the cliffs like waterfalls rustling in the cold wind. Even the bird life looked grey. A grey heron on the bank, grey pigeons cooing on the ledges, grey sparrows squabbling in the grey balls of flotsam, caught among great grey fallen trees.

On a narrow-necked promontory, formed by a curve in the river, we could see the roofless remnants of St James Church. Linked to Cistercian monks who founded Tintern Abbey, a high number of medicinal herbs have been found in the grounds, including the non-native elecampane used to treat respiratory ailments. It is speculated that it had been a leper colony. There was no prospect of landing on this last leg. The speed at which we were propelled was astonishing.

The sky opened up for our last stint as we approached the awe-inspiring sight of Chepstow Castle, whose gently ruinous turrets and battlements seem to grow directly out of the rock to become an extension of the cliff face. The sun was behind the castle, flashing through window openings and between lofty towers. We had to put our hands above our eyes and narrow them to appreciate the splendour ahead. We drifted without paddling. The tide was increasingly strong; we had to keep head-on with the flow.

There was just one bend before the town and we knew that there should be a pontoon floating before the modern road bridge. I imagined missing the pontoon and not having the power to back-paddle against the tide and being swept into the confluence of the Severn where Davy Jones's locker must surely await. That or death by mud. We pulled up easily on the pontoon and secured the kayaks.

We had completed our second trip. We pulled together for a photo, cheerfully taken by a passer-by. We were smiling and filthy. Life was good. We looked back at the pontoon, where twenty minutes earlier we had landed. The pontoon had dropped 2 metres in this time. The gangplank to the pontoon had become steep. Water is dangerous. Treat with respect.

CHAPTER 4

SCOTLAND COAST TO COAST

You only see a rainbow with your back to the sun

The light in Scotland is different. It reveals colour in a more vibrant way than the light in England. The St Ives artists insisted that the light was special in Cornwall, and Turner thought that the light in Margate was the best anywhere. Cornwall and Thanet have water on three sides, which would explain part of this, and Cornwall, with the prevailing wind from the Atlantic, is likely to have less pollution. Only Scotland, for me, shows an appreciable difference. With so much moisture in the air, it isn't the clarity. It is something else. I've seen it in New Zealand and in Iceland. Snowscapes have their own strange light, but on this journey, there was no snow. A fair bit of drizzle, but still the light is memorable in its vivacity.

The Great Glen is a deep straight fissure that runs at forty-five degrees through the middle of Scotland, as if there had been an attempt to decapitate the country with a giant sword. The glen runs from Fort William in the southwest to Inverness in the northeast. I've never had a grasp of Scotland's history, but it is clearly violent, tribal, and proud. The glen has towns at each end, and the middle, that start with 'Fort-', a fair clue to the military strategic importance of the route: William, George, and Augusta respectively. The history is richly coloured by their own language and culture.

We had planned to start at Oban, follow the coast up to Fort William, then traverse the Great Glen through the Caledonian Canal and Loch Ness and the River Ness to Inverness, and finish with a sea trip up the Moray Firth to Cromarty.

We had hired equipment from a dour Yorkshireman who had established a successful outdoor adventure business nearby. It's a long way for us and we weren't on the water in our three single kayaks until three thirty in the afternoon of that day in June.

Mark had photocopied a series of maps, which he had neatly laminated. He had notes on expected arrival times with accurate tidal information laid out. The problem with this was that once we were behind schedule, it became difficult to keep pace with where we were. Near the entrance to the sea on the northern end of our trip, we were caught out by this with near disaster.

Oban is an attractive small town on the Firth of Lorn. The bay is a perfect horseshoe shape. Perhaps this would be good luck for us? The town and the coastal route that we took up to Fort William, where we change from seagoing to

SCOTLAND
COAST TO COAST
N
W
E
S
13TH - 21ST JUNE 2014
111 MILES
NESSIE!
BEEP!
BEEP!
BEEP!
MIDGE APP
!!!!
12-mile day
Loch Oich
Loch Lochy
CORPACH
Great Glen
10-mile day
Loch Linnhe
FORT WILLIAM
Ben Nevis
ONICH
Atlantic Ocean
PORT APPIN
GLENCOE
7-mile day
18-mile day
OBAN
START
CAMP
CANAL

ROSEMARKIE
FORTROSE
FINISH
North Sea
8-mile day
3-mile day
INVERNESS
GOLDEN EAGLE
18-mile day
GREAT SCOT!
17-mile day
GREAT GLEN!
Loch Ness
Canoe Trail
Caledonian Canal Plans
T. Telford
FORT AUGUSTUS
18-mile day
Loch Ness
B*!@☠!!
S
NI
I
W
E
F
Dave Chisholm FRGS
10
20
30
40
MILES

inland water, is well protected from the ravages of the Northern Atlantic and the westerly winds by the Isle of Mull and later by the mountains of the Morvern and Ardgour peninsula.

The air was full of drizzle. We were quickly saturated. The sea was very calm, and the oily-looking reflections rolled around us with the surface of the sea smooth and appearing unbroken. The rain cleared after an hour and the low sun highlighted distant snow-capped mountains in all directions. We were all a little in awe. We had planned to cross the broad Ardmucknish Bay, five miles north, before setting up for the night.

The evening was echoing with the call of oystercatchers. We were passing the heads of seals bobbing in the water that looked as friendly as my neighbour's Labrador. Sandpipers and redshank skimmed close to the water level while white gulls flapped above them like puppets.

We arrived at a promontory at the southern end of the bay. The ruined Dunstaffnage Castle, moss and ivy clad, peered at us through the trees. We rolled onto the stony beach and wandered up to the castle for a closer look. Forlorn and hard, we wondered about the tough life of former inhabitants. The weather and the landscape give the Scots their tough image. Looking at the unforgiving granite walls in the grey wind, I felt happy enough being born a southern English softie.

We had to decide if we were going to hug the coast around the bay, or save six miles by heading out two miles over open water to an inlet called Camas Nathais. It was calm and we had not exerted ourselves much so far. We were, by design, heading towards the main body of Loch Linnhe on an incoming tide, so we took a vote, and we all went for the open-water crossing option.

We kept close together. We had little experience in open water and there was some trepidation. Mark had carefully equipped us with flares in case of emergency and we had practised all manner of kayak rescue in the event of capsize. For hardened seafaring folk, it probably would have been described as a pleasant gentle swell with light choppiness. Wind is the enemy of the kayaker, and we had a headwind that rudely threw water into our faces for the forty minutes it took to cross over. I was surprised how huge a gentle swell appears when right on top of it at water level. It has an unchallengeable quality, like riding a massive beast. Confidence quickly grew and all was well.

We beached up on a sandy inlet surrounded by rock pools with the thin clear look of gin. We hauled our boats onto the heather and took off wet spray decks and waterproofs. The wind had dropped to an evening calm and the clouds had scudded by, revealing a welcome red orb of dying sun that had just enough warmth to dry things off. The seaweed had formed a crunchy, comfortable seat for us. There were yellow flag irises lining the miniature banks of a tiny stream that trickled onto the sand and disappeared. In front of the tough scrub of stunted trees that covered the hills all around, there was a profusion of ragged robin blooms, like a thousand exploding pink butterflies, leaving tatty remnants of wings among the rich green grass. I collected hundreds of winkles from the pools that were arranged in strata formation, like fingers reaching into the sea. Dave lit a fire and built a simple driftwood tripod to suspend our aluminium pot full of winkles. You need a lot of winkles to make a mouthful. Mark had produced a few paper clips that we could use to ease the sweet curly molluscs from their black shells. Lounging around without much to do, grazing on winkles is a fine thing, but if you're hungry, not ideal. We had plenty of bread to fill up on. A winkle is a univalve so is not a filter feeder, like bivalves, so it is safer to eat. Because of the pervading cleanliness of the whole area and the sea, we agreed that we could eat any shellfish that we could forage. There is no light pollution on the west coast of Scotland, and we all noticed the blackness above, the dazzle of the prominent stars, and the milkiness of the millions of others deeper into space, flung across the sky like spilt sugar.

✼

Dave had a morning dip each day and thought nothing of sliding into the bone-numbing water at any time. The water never warms up here to a temperature that normal people would want to tolerate. Mark and I managed to join Dave just a few times for this masochistic madness. There is a thrill and rising warmth like a stiff whisky running through your veins when it's all over, but I'm not sure the suffering is worth it. People all over the cold world do this by tradition. There must be something to it. The cold, clean water, to Dave, is as natural as snow is to a yeti.

Mark had found a sheep skull with horns attached and placed it like a figurehead under the deck netting at the front of his boat. At the end of this journey, we were to inscribe the skull, in ink, with our journey details and our names and we would present it to the landlord of The Anderson in Rosemarkie, who would display it in his bar. And it was still there when I visited a year later.

We followed the coast up a narrowing channel between the mainland and Lismore Island. We had planned our timing to meet Port Appin at slack tide. Shortly after settling into a comfortable paddle routine, we noticed a sheltered bay with a long shallow beach behind, and a group of three people working in waders in the shallows. I was curious about this aquaculture and led the three of us to see if we could chat with these workers at this early time of day. I wanted to ask what they were farming. We came within 50 metres of the group, which seemed to comprise a grey-haired man and two younger individuals: a man and a woman. Perhaps father and children. I called to say good morning and they either pretended that they didn't hear or were deliberately snubbing my greeting. I couldn't believe it. I asked what they were farming, and drifted a bit closer. Nothing. 'Are they oyster trestles you're working with?' I enquired, hoping to have a bit of to and fro about my hometown fame of Whitstable. They didn't lift their heads for a second, but the patriarch replied with a curt yes.

'Fine morning,' Mark offered. No answer. We looked at each other with a mental 'fuck off then' as we back-paddled, leaving the miserable trio to their work.

The slightly constricting channel and the flowing tide caused strong currents to start rolling beneath us like a pan of water just before boiling. The swell grew and we were careful to avoid the larger whirlpools that appeared here and there. I could see from the bent-down concentration of Mark and Dave's kayak body language that minds were focused. We were through the pinch point speedily at Port Appin, and calm again returned.

There were a lot of eider ducks bobbing on the choppiness. They are sleek-looking, large ducks. Their name is flung about in the bedding world, but I doubt that most would give a thought to the reality of these beautifully marked wild birds. Several had young with them. There were guillemots, who spend the winter out at sea, fishing here near the coast to feed their young. They continually disappeared underwater, only to resurface 30 metres away, emerging with vigilant, darting eyes. We identified another auk in the loch: the razorbill. On the water they have the look of divers. We came across red-throated divers further up the loch. Their long plaintive cries were a common sound up to Fort William. By tradition, the red-throated diver is called the 'rain goose' and is said to indicate fine weather with short cries and wet weather with long cries. I mentioned this to the boys and Mark pointed out that they couldn't go wrong with Scottish weather that changes all the time!

The mineral scent of the sea was more marked when we were further off the coast. The coastline has its own smells, characterised by the seaweed and flotsam that was a more complex brew. Light rain with bright sun followed us for some time and the hills were washing over with transparent grey curtains. Turning slightly landward, we were paddling towards the rising sun, so it was some time before any of us noticed that a perfect rainbow was arcing behind us. From our position, it appeared to spring up from the hills on the edge of one side of the loch and finish neatly on the other side like an enormous multicoloured tied arch bridge. You can miss much by concentrating only on the direction of travel, and treasure is to be found in the less obvious places. The sun is the source of all-natural light, but looking towards the sun will not reveal what is the perfect display of the interaction of light and colour: you only see a rainbow with your back to the sun.

After a few miles we saw the powerful sight of Castle Stalker, which is a plain rectangular block of a place with a heavy stone external staircase to the main door. It is built on an island. Paddling in close to the small island, the water became very shallow. We climbed out of our boats and pulled them onto water that was only three inches deep, then left them to march up close to the impressive edifice. No one was at home, and we couldn't tell if it was a private home or open to the public. Dave climbed the stairs and peered through one of the windows. His assessment was that it looked like a home. We didn't know if we were welcome so began to walk back to the kayaks.

The tide had continued without concern from us, but the three-inch depth of water had now become a foot. The boats were all drifting out to sea with all our equipment on board. We looked at each other and by silent acknowledgement were kicking each other's imaginary arses in horror. No fault came into the equation. I made a quick mental assessment of what I had on board: wallet, passport, clothes, sleeping bag, the lot. The boats were about 50 metres away and the wind was rocking the unoccupied craft and turning the bows away from the wind. The cockpits were not even covered, spray decks had been loosely thrown onto the kayaks carelessly, and paddles placed into the foot area, with one end proud and catching the wind.

We would have to swim for them. 'Take off what you want and load me up. Swim for your life,' I told Dave and Mark. I would hold onto the kit. They both stripped off at least some clothes as if in a race. Dave's arms were struggling to free themselves of silky Lycra sleeves, shaking them frantically. They half ran and half waded towards the stricken vessels with steps lifted artificially high to avoid the drag of wading. 'Bollocks, bollocks, bollocks...,' was the general refrain. The terrain under the foot-deep water was rocky and uneven. The boys wore Neoprene footwear that had only a thin sole. There were deep channels in the rock, ideal to snap bones. I was worried. *Slow down, we're not going to die.* The nearer of the kayaks seemed to have snagged on something and was stationary.

'If you can get that one, you can use it to chase down the others,' I said, annoyingly stating the obvious.

To my relief, the water didn't seem to be deepening as I watched Dave, now 50 metres away, hobble-wading remorselessly. Like you would expect in any good film, as Dave bore down on the kayak, the snagged kayak suddenly freed itself and was again drifting out to sea. Mark unexpectedly completely disappeared underwater. He'd dropped into some kind of hole but was back on the shallow seabed almost immediately. The drop had broken his hope and he put his hands on both knees and stood still. All the kayaks suddenly changed direction and were being blown inland. The near resignation changed to hope, and in one long minute, Dave was on the first of our boats, had jumped in, and was going towards the others, quickly, with purpose. He hadn't had to swim. Dave held on to the deck rope that we always have surrounding our boats and he brought them in. Dave's smile looked like his face would split. We couldn't contain our joy. We slapped each other's backs, and we slapped the sea. If we had been a retreating force from a failed attempt to lay siege to the castle, we would have been slaughtered in that shallow sea. Lesson learned.

⁂

We pushed onwards, keeping close to the southern shore, looking for a place to brew tea and the chance to collect our thoughts. We stopped at a sheltered bay nestled neatly along the rocky coast. The general terrain had been for a while a kind of very low cliff that dropped straight into the water. At this tiny beach we found bright red sea urchins and a similarly coloured starfish among the kelp and wrack on the rocks. The sea had the feeling of edible abundance, and the occasional working trawler chugged by.

We had a second open-water decision to make when ahead was a shallow bay with an outreaching promontory that we could head straight towards and cut off distance. The sea swell was trickier at a forty-five-degree angle, and rolling in from behind, so we wouldn't be able to see exactly when we might be pushed sideways. The waves were up to a metre in height. We chose again to set off on the mile across open water to this promontory. The going is tougher further out to sea and any long distances offshore with Scotland's unpredictable weather were to be avoided. Halfway through the crossing, wave direction altered enough so that the waves were right behind us and we could bury the nose of our kayaks in the trough ahead, so planting the body of the boat in such a way that we could surf along, then repeat on the next wave.

We decided to visit one of the small islands about a mile offshore and comfortably made the trip over to Eilean Balnagowan. The island is two lumps of rock, each about ten acres, joined by a sandy isthmus. We were greeted by the deafening screeching of hundreds of gulls. The least prevalent gull in the UK is, surprisingly, the common gull and Scotland is their stronghold. We had chanced upon a small colony. It was June, so there was a mixture of small chicks and eggs in the many nests that were collected on the slightly higher ground above the beach. The communal mobbing of predators makes nesting in colonies safer for gulls than lone nests. We were not mobbed relentlessly; they seemed to tolerate us walking quite close. We were anxious not to disturb them, so didn't dilly-dally. We set off on our last leg of the day.

We reached a sheltered beach to camp just before Kentallen Bay. We could see that we were near to Ballachulish, so we decided to walk into the village. We found a place to eat and joined noisy locals watching football on a bar screen. England v Italy. Great cheers roared when Italy scored, with energetic fist-shaking in the air or banging on tables. We weren't sure if we were safe as more and more beer went down. They must have known that we were English. England scored. We said nothing, just smirked at each other quietly. Most of all this was good-humoured, but I felt that it was just as well that Italy won the game, and we were allowed to be on our way unscathed.

It wasn't far from midsummer's day, so daylight lingered for our walk back at eleven. We had been prepared for the evil midges, but so far, we had been free of them. Back at the kayaks, we noticed the first few, so we covered all skin with nets and gloves. There was a chill wind and bed beckoned. The call of seabirds at night is occasional but dramatic. Eerie wails drifted in the still air that set the tone for the dreams of a light sleep.

We had Ben Nevis in view through day three, and we had camped close to Glen Coe. The beauty of the bigger landscape was everywhere. Today's tidal timings were critical. The loch quickly constricts from a mile wide to two hundred metres. The speed of flow through Corran Narrows, only two miles on, can be 8 knots.

There had already been a few salmon farms along the way and this section of the loch seemed to host many. The economic benefits of this farming are huge. Scottish salmon is the largest of any food export in the UK. The environmental drawbacks are, however, not so good to the wild salmon population, and damages marine life on the seabed. Watching the small boats chugging back and forth at their work on the mid-loch enclosures, however, looked like a peaceful way to spend a working day.

We slid up the sandy beach of a caravan camp just before the Narrows at Inchree. We had a bit of time to waste so called at their little shop for a few supplies. The woman who served us had a tall pile of silver hair balanced on her head. She had a soft and lilting highland accent, but was not a cheerful type. We told her that we were heading north through the narrow channel and her response was, 'I wouldn't if I were you. You probably won't make it'.

We're doomed, we were all thinking as we avoided eye contact with each other. Dave spent most of that day imitating her words. 'I wouldn't if I were you' in a Scottish accent became the go-to phrase when danger might be ahead.

At the turn of tide, we paddled through the still water with no effort. We crossed over to the north side for the rest of the day. The ferry was docked on the south side and a sturdy white lighthouse stood reassuringly opposite. Passing the small village, it was noticeable that grey and white were the colours of everything. The houses were low - except for the two-storey Inn at Ardgour - and they were generally painted white with grey slate roofs. The walls and harbour architecture were grey stone. The water was grey with white frothy caps on the chop. The sky was a shifting landscape of grey and white. The distant mountains were greys that diminished to dull white in the far foggy distance. I pointed this out to the boys and suggested that if we had watched the football in the Inn at Ardgour on the shore here, it would have been on a black and white TV. I imagined a plate of fresh mackerel with the grey-blue markings of a Scottish evening sky.

The shoreline continued to be rocks diving steeply into the sea. Not all is grey, and change happens quickly. After the next six miles, where we made an early camp, there were four bands of colour to the shore. The lower section was a pale faun, like a rabbit's back, where the rocks had spent most of their life submerged, had little seaweed on them, and had a whiteish bloom from barnacles, or it was sandy with larger particle size than further towards the sea. The next band was a 3- or 4-metre width of black, with a slight green hue, like a starling's plumage, flecked with a very pale raw umber and violet, indicating the height of tidal movement where seaweed clung to everything. This was followed by a metre width of clean rocks with no vegetation. Here was a pleasing russet red with some cream elements, like a wet fox. Above this, it is all greens, until distance and precipitation in all its forms greys the vista.

The route was comfortable with a slight wind behind. The sun eventually beamed down on us as we unpacked on a flat area where a stream met the loch with a direct view of Ben Nevis. The mountain has just sixty days in the year when its summit is not cloud-covered and today was one of those days.

We all spent time on the usual activities of sponging out water from the boats, hanging up what we could to dry, and repacking our various dry bags to make access good for whatever we might need in the evening.

Dave stripped off and swam far out into the loch. 'Nutter,' Mark commented. Dave pushed on through the pristine waters of the sea into the evening sun, more like a paddle steamer than a seal, making it look comfortable and easy.

Mark had dried off and perched on a rock on higher ground towards the bracken and brush. With his pince-nez perched on his nose in the same manner, he looked like the Tailor of Gloucester on a bobbin. He was writing his journal. It has been a joy to read Mark's notes from the field, and he is the one that perseveres with this. Mark also makes notes on what equipment might be useful next time, and on possible refinements to existing kit. All useful later.

I had brought a small set of watercolours and a nine-inch block of cartridge paper, so I set about trying to record this majestic view of Ben Nevis, with his regal ermine cape of snow on his shoulders. I spent a long time at this, but I had not painted with watercolour, and not outside, for many years. I like the Norwich School, and I had imagined a delicate wash of clean colours, creating depth and drama like a John Sell Cotman masterpiece. Maybe a few rainwater marks would be dotted about to add some authenticity to the en plein air look. My lofty ambition resulted in the landscape equivalent of a portrait artist's smiley face emoji on a stick man. The paints didn't appear again.

The evening was again on the cold side of cool, so we huddled round our evening fire and went through what we had done so far and reconfirmed our anticipated journey plan. We tended to do this every evening. Once chat had ceased, we settled down for the night – me first, as usual. There was the drowsy lapping of the sea and the occasional haunting nighttime wail of sea birds, but also an incessant croaking of frogs that reverberated all night, like a flatulent motorbike on low revs.

The morning saw us attempting to make simple bread on the camp fire that was still embers at seven o'clock. We had stunningly clear weather that was dazzlingly bright. I laid out pancakes of dough to cook directly on the flat hot rocks around the fire, and wrapped a rolled plain dough sausage around a stick braced on two catapult-shaped stays over the heat. It was edible, even quite good with hot beans. The idea was, that carrying plain flour and a bit of dried yeast and salt already mixed would be weight efficient, just needing the addition of some water to use. It might have been – but I was still carrying the bag of flour at the end.

The water had the faintest movement on its reflective surface, like old float glass. The mountains in the water were indistinguishable from the mountains in the air and burst with a singing vibrancy. A linnet perched on a gorse branch nearby and sang out with equal clarity. The Victorians prized them as cage birds because of their song. Our friend here would have a better life.

We had all washed off the salt by bathing in the stream next to our camp. The 'burn', as I ought to call it, tumbled down the rocks and spread like a mini river delta in many tiny watercourses to enter the loch. A fallen branch had made a perfect pool just above high-water mark. There were tadpoles in some of the still ponds to each side. I had found a newt in one of these and brought it to the boys to photograph. There are only three types of newt in Scotland, and although this was a juvenile, it looked like it could only be a great crested newt. In my world, newts and bats can stop building developers in their tracks. 'You can't build a house here,' it told me as I let it slide off my hand onto the damp margins of the burn.

Our closest relationships are built and strengthened by touch. It is true of nature. When surrounding yourself with any natural environment, staying physically close to that environment will strengthen your love for it. The feel of things is an ever-changing experience. The feel of grainy hard rock will be cool, but with a soft coat of lichen, the heat is drawn from your palm more slowly. The soft yielding mud around your ankles or the crispy dryness of bracken on your legs, the spongy wetness of moss, the firmness of wet sand, the delicacy of a beetle on your forearm or the surprising weight of that fleshy newt. We are closely aware of our environment on our river journeys and you can't help but be aware of the feel of things. As you are physically touched by nature, you learn what you can trust, what you enjoy and how to best navigate your way. Your interactions are constant and you build intimacy.

What you learn from touch in an outdoor environment is important in many ways. For some, your life might depend on it. Mark explains here what 'feel' can mean for climbing:

Climbers become aware of each rock type's characteristics and how they are different from each other. Limestone from sandstone, slate from granite. Its likelihood to have edges, pockets, its grip, and its ability to dry quickly or be brittle and snap. To be able to climb well on slate doesn't mean you will climb well on gritstone, or vice versa, as the techniques are different, because each rock presents differently.

Assessing what you are up against before committing helps calm the mind, allows you to choose your rack of gear for protection when clipping in to the rope, whether to expect small or wide cracks, and if they would hold well enough. Weathered rock tends to have rounded edges whereas quarried or fallen cliff faces are cleaved with reassuring edges to wrap fingers around or balance toes on.

I have two rocks on my desk. One is sandstone worn by the action of a glacial stream, rounded but with coarse texture. It has clearly visible layers of old sediment. The other is quartzite, and is angular and rough with sharp edges. Why do I have a couple of odd stones on my desk? Stones are stones, right? Not to me. They break up my day. I will turn one in my hand, feeling its texture and grippiness, and it returns me to a distant place, to events, to friends, to long hard days far from the workings of an office. I might remember the bottom of a sea cliff with the sound of waves and sea birds, or perhaps the narrow focus of a single hard move that's needed high on a remote crag out of sight of all the world, including the second when your concentration is entirely on what your finger pads tell you of a tiny piece of rock. You have to know everything about that rock – its slightly scooped surface, its granularity, and its fixture to the greater cliff face.

What you know about the feel of snow and ice when climbing is vital. That terrain has changeable qualities, which need to be assessed on the day. They can change overnight or during the course of a warm day. It can be too brittle or too soft. Your assessment of its ability to hold weight can tip the safety margin equation. I find myself returning from a climbing trip, assessing stone walls in the street, running my hands over the grains within, determining the friction from their sloping surfaces. Could I pull on it? It's a bit quirky, but if you're committing to this kind of activity, this regularly sizing up is a good habit.

The last of the west coast up to the entrance to the Caledonian Canal was only an hour or so. Jellyfish were suddenly everywhere. These were lion's mane jellyfish and Dave was well aware of the potential danger of their sting. The giant of the species, common on Scotland's west coast but not present among this bloom, can trail tentacles for tens of metres and are particularly dangerous.

We gratefully absorbed the blazing sunshine as we glided comfortably past Fort William and beached at Corpach. My arms had a salty covering like the yeasty bloom of a Victoria plum. The next salt water would be the North Sea.

※

We had arranged to check in with our boat hire man, whose office was here, but he was out for an hour. So we decided to call in at a hotel nearby. We had stepped into 1976. A shoddy, pale matchboard-clad bar trimmed with Formica stood on one side of the room with shiny PVC seating on a dirty vinyl floor. The pink-striped walls were adorned with chocolate-box paintings and sign-written mirrors advertising long-gone brands of beer. Bulbous, brass-trimmed lighting glared down from the ceiling. We ought to be smelling of Brut, swigging Double Diamond and chatting to girls in short skirts on stilts drinking Babycham. We were the only customers. Spam wasn't on the menu, so we made do with eggs and ham.

When we returned to the equipment hire HQ, our Yorkshire friend generously offered to run us up Neptune's Staircase, where Telford's engineered series of eight locks elevates substantial-sized craft 20 metres above sea level. This saved a lot of time and effort. Avoiding the carrying of our boats and all our equipment up the hill was a great bonus.

The eventual realisation of the Caledonian Canal was the conception of Thomas Telford. The route of the canal had been mooted as long ago as 1620 but was not fully in operation until 1822 after nineteen years of heavy work. Connecting Loch Linnhe to the Moray Firth would make for a much faster and safer journey between the east and west coasts of Scotland. Before its opening, any ship wanting to travel from Glasgow to Edinburgh had to either undertake the long journey around southern England or take the more perilous voyage around Scotland's north coast. Unfortunately, the canal was outdated by the time it was completed – and at twice the anticipated cost. Investors in the canal made a massive loss. Ships were becoming ever larger as steel hulls became prevalent. The draft capacity of the canal had already been reduced from twenty to fifteen feet to reduce cost, and these larger vessels, including most of the Navy, were never able to utilise the short cut.

The canal on this first section is an even channel with defined banks and runs alongside the River Lochy to Loch Lochy. Once on the canal, the feel of the water was noticeable straight away. Fresh water feels and smells different from the saline mix we had got used to. The function of our boats barely changed, but it took some time adjusting to the new normality. One way or another, when travelling by canoe, you are always in direct contact with the water.

In the low-lying land, there was a small amount of farmland. The distinctive coconut-vanilla scent of flowering gorse hung in the air. Mature deciduous trees dotted the route, rustling overhead. There were meadows whose margins near woods were decorated with pink stands of foxglove and the medieval blue of viper's bugloss. Painted lady and peacock butterflies made their jigging dance around these pollen factories to a rhythmless beat. The electric buzz of the bumble bee carried on the breeze. Lizards basked on warm rocks. Three friends paddled quietly.

We've encountered a few swing bridges on our travels. At Gairlochy, not far southwest of the lock, there is a small but neat white-painted iron swing bridge over the canal. The bridge allows cars access on the B road above, or it will be swung open, allowing river craft passage along the waterway. The primary supporting structure for any sizeable swing bridge is a vertical locating pin and support ring, which need to be near the centre of gravity. On smaller swing bridges like this one, the pivot is on one end and opens in the way a gate would operate.

We carried our boats around Gairlochy Lock and were very soon into the expansive Gairlochy Loch. We kept to the northern bank and tied up at the base of an open glade of beech trees. We set camp as the light softened. The evening sun pierced the thin canopy in long shards, highlighting the rolling dust. The ground was crunchy with the satisfying sound of empty dried beech nut shells. I found a number of chanterelle mushrooms. These have a distinctive and appetising aroma of apricots. We fried them in a pan of onions with our meal.

Two bright yellow dragonflies settled on the yellow-red parts of one of the boats. These were golden-ringed dragonflies, and they are one of Britain's largest. They have huge bright green eyes and the black and yellow of their bodies is a combination of colours that often spells danger in the animal world. They are voracious predators and feast on insects almost their own size, including other dragonflies. One of these had a slight club shape to its abdomen, which identified it as male. These insects look for a place to lay their eggs at this time of year. They have evolved to seek a particular pattern of polarised light that is found on the right kind of water for them to lay their eggs. The reflective light from vehicles, especially red ones, apparently, and various other man-made objects, such as our boats, can confuse the beasts. The dragonflies were in the same place in the morning.

We had all purchased a midge app on our phones. This useful information forecasts where and when to expect midges on a daily basis on a scale of one (midge-free) to five (midges out in force). The midge forecast for this spot that day was three. It soon became apparent that it was accurate. The lower the light, the more we were slapping any bare skin. We fully covered up any flesh with face nets and gloves. A full 40,000 midges can land on one unprotected arm! Our protection saved us the nightmare of death by a million stings, but it was too hot. The nylon fabric of the netting was as comfortable as the nylon sheets would have been in the bedrooms of the Corpach Hotel. Sleep was fitful.

*

We kept on all midge gear right through packing up in the early morning. It was not just me that needed the trowel, but we all avoided exposing these bigger parts of flesh until the midge app gave us the thumbs-up. Once a fair distance from the shore, it was safe to strip off, and we paddled on into another bright day.

The overall impression of the loch with its steep banks was ominous. Even on the brightest day imaginable, there is a blackness to the water and a heaviness to the steep wooded banks on either side. This presence stayed with me throughout the canal sections and the feeling deepened through Loch Oich, which is narrower.

We thought it wise to wait some time for the midges to disappear, then we decided to moor up for trowel use. The deciduous trees had given way to Forestry Commission plantations of conifers, and we picked a landing place where the banks didn't rise steeply but were flatter and had level ground where we could walk. We all secured our boats, and I set off in one direction with the necessary kit while the boys wandered into the trees.

When I returned to the boats, the boys were some way off and beckoning me excitedly to join them further into the woods. Approaching them, I could see what their interest was. In the grey-brown acidic and moribund landscape, always under pine plantations, there were strange and shamanic-like collections of dolls and teddy bears. Many looked like they had spent a winter there and were bedraggled, with stuffing emerging from failed seams, and had signs of moss growing on them. Others looked like they had recently been placed there. There were collections of teddies and dolls at tea parties, beneath mini umbrellas or tucked up in mini beds. Some were small and some substantial. We hardly talked to each other. We continued to explore. Many were hung from trees. The site of this creepy collection covered about 50 by 50 metres. All the toys had been displayed in happy situations, which detracted from the pervading sense of witchcraft. It reminded me of stumbling upon remote vegetable gardens in the West African bush, where there might be an inner tube with feathers stuck on it, raised on a stick in a juju warning display. The dolls had overtones of voodoo with staring eyes. Maybe if we looked closely, they would all be lanced with needles. Although this is a remote location, the Great Glen Way is nearby and by the look of the ground and tracks, it had been often visited. We saw nobody and jumped back in our boats, hoping that we had not been cursed for ever.

We would later hear several different stories about this place. The internet has a small amount to say on it, but no explanation of why it is there or who is doing it all. I understand, however, that the woods have since been logged and the 'shrine' has gone. The landlord of a later-visited pub told us that he believed a terminally ill woman had gone to these woods to die, leaving her small child in care, to spare the child seeing her mother's unhappy decline. She decorated the place as a shrine to her child, expecting death. Death never came. She returned to live a normal life, reunited with her child, but felt that a woodland spirit had cured her. She had continued offering these talisman tokens in thanks for the miracle that she believed she had experienced. The landlord told the tale in such a way that it seemed he had recounted this story many times. It's probably nonsense.

We had been on the lookout for golden eagles, and we were to have several sightings that day. They are not strongly territorial but have what is called a home range, which covers tens of square miles, so we may have seen the same eagle a few times. The southern side of the loch is less wooded and not as steep. We were too low to enjoy views beyond the slopes either side of the loch, so we did not have the feeling of being surrounded by substantial mountains. We had seen buzzards circling overhead at all locations, but we saw emerging from behind the southern horizon a solitary raptor that appeared to be too large. A golden eagle is about the size of a flying door. At the distance we observed him, we couldn't be sure. We were willing the bird to drift our way. We had one small set of binoculars and Mark had them with him. The bird was edging closer all the time. He had not made a single wing beat, which ticks a box for ID. If it's not a buzzard, then it's our eagle. Buzzards have a longer body compared to their wings. The main clue came by looking above the opposite shore. Here there were several buzzards clearly a similar distance from us that gave us the confirmation that the eagle on the southern side was much larger. A golden eagle is twice the size of a buzzard. The other factor that helps is my own experience of watching golden eagles in the previous year on Mull, where I had been to see the enormous white-tailed eagle.

Bird watching can be like collecting. It can become about ticking off species. A counting game. In time, even those who start their ornithological journey in this way become overtaken with the bigger appreciation and mystery of birds. A golden eagle is a fine view, but it is made greater with the knowledge of the power of the bird and the folklore surrounding Scotland's most famous raptor.

We negotiated a lock into a short section of canal before entering Loch Oich after another swing bridge. We were quickly at the Well of Seven Heads where there is a well-known monument depicting seven decapitated heads, a grisly memorial of an event that reminds us of Scotland's bloodthirsty inter-clan feuding of past centuries. We stopped here at a café that offered an easy break.

Loch Oich was a spectacular vista in front of us. This is the high point between the coasts. More like a river than a loch, being very narrow at only just over half a mile wide at its widest point and four miles long. It is fed by the River Garry near Invergarry and is connected to Loch Ness, seven miles northeast by the river Oich.

The banks have fewer sterile coniferous plantations than many parts of the Highlands. Running up to the water's edge are deciduous and mixed woodland with steep meadows dotted with gorse and rocky outcrops. The afternoon air was pleasantly fragrant with a faint scent of pruning blackcurrants.

It was the middle of the salmon fishing season. We hadn't gone to the trouble and expense of obtaining a licence or permission, but when we next stopped, Mark and I both tried spinning for whatever might bite using our tiny telescopic rods. Salmon fishing, like salmon farming, is big business in Scotland with estates employing expert ghillies that guide fee-paying guests to best enjoy the salmon and other game on their particular estate. I've fished at least some of the time on all our kayak journeys and sometimes I can actually see the fish pointing and laughing at me. We would all waste away if we were to rely on my fishing haul to feed us.

We finished quite early for the day and set up on a meadow just beyond the end of Loch Oich. The warmth returned, but not the midges. We could have chosen an onward route through the River Oich to Loch Ness for the next day, where there are some grade two rapids to negotiate, but we decided on the canal.

The river begins a more natural route as it leaves the loch. Here there is a spectacular bridge that at a glance looks like any other suspension bridge. It is now a footbridge only but was built and designed for heavier traffic in 1854 by James Dredge. He had invented the taper suspension bridge. The principle is that of a double cantilever bridge. Each half is self-supporting and the deck is not supported by rods from a cable slung between two supporting towers as in a traditional suspension bridge. Each half-deck is suspended on angled chains from a tapered main chain that hangs from the top of the tower and is attached to the outer end of the half-deck. The term 'taper principle' comes from the fact that the number of links stacked across the chain are incrementally reduced the further it gets from the supporting tower. The design is lighter and cheaper to build than a traditional suspension bridge. The impression is airy and elegant.

You have to wonder at the feat involved in building these kinds of structures so far from centres of population when transport was so much more difficult, and all this technology was recent. Victorian Britain was crammed with people of great ability, confidence and ambition that brought change and innovation to the world. Providing solutions that meet the challenges caused largely by the industrialisation of these past visionaries must be the main challenge for visionaries of the future.

Before dusk descended, we took a walk together on the other side of the bridge. The low sun highlighted a haze of dry particles drifting above the thistles in the hay meadow that we were wading through. A background hum of insects and the scent of poppies gave a drowsy note to the evening. We emerged through a gorse thicket into a second meadow. As we stood quietly looking over the river, a barn owl, very near, unhurriedly flapped by directly in front of us like a giant moth.

The owl was scanning the grass from a height of 2 metres. The impression was white, but he had a mottled caramel back, like dried bracken under a gauze veil, slubbed with dark knots. The effect of this pattern creates a slight vibrating effect on the eye and makes it difficult to focus upon.

A barn owl is a silent and lethal assassin. They have finely engineered features, with tiny serrations on their feathers that act as a damper to deaden sound. Velvety down over its body absorbs more sound. Their face is a concave heart that funnels sound towards its large ear openings. They have finely acute hearing, which is adapted to locate the position of their prey below. They can swoop for a kill with pinpoint accuracy – even in the pitch dark.

An owl has a mysterious aura. It floats in the air like pollen. When close, their appearance in flight has the strange still quietness of falling snow. The owl silenced the insects. It silenced the meadow, and it silenced the breeze. For a glimpse of time, all action faltered; a spell had been cast. We were listening to silence.

The hunter and the hunted evolve together. Do the mice sense this silence before the owl strikes? Once caught, the hapless victim will hang helplessly from curved rapier talons until landed on some fence post where he will be slowly dismembered. His last sight in life, the passionless gaze of the predator.

The owl didn't linger and was soon in the distance, where it was methodically quartering the field and soon set off to terrorise the mammal life in another meadow.

With no midges on day six, Dave was able to take his morning dip before we set off for the much larger body of water which is Loch Ness. The seven miles to Fort Augustus saw a few motorised pleasure boats cruise by, occupied by holidaymakers, who all greeted us cheerfully. The canal is an attractive run for this section, with trees on grassy banks and occasional walkers on the towpath to one side.

There is a series of locks at Fort Augustus, and this was a lengthy haul of the boats for us, but we stopped in the town for a rest and a snack. It is a honeypot tourist destination and was busy with people doing very little. People of all ages were walking about aimlessly in the chill summer wind, eating ice cream, and peering at window displays of cardigans and whisky. The coach park was full. We were looking at happy people away from their daily lives. They were looking at three blokes getting wet and sleeping rough.

This was the psychological halfway point for us, and it was satisfying to be in the meat of our voyage, setting off to take on Loch Ness. The wind was against us, and waves were increasing. The going was slow. Mergansers were in large numbers on the water with at least one red-throated diver bobbing around us. A sparrowhawk harried and mobbed a buzzard overhead. The spray was in our face, and we set a zig-zag course to keep the waves either behind or in front of us. We decided to keep to the south-eastern side. As Fort Augustus disappeared behind us, the banks became steep and rocky with some spectacularly large Douglas fir trees breaking through the deciduous canopy. We spent some time very close to the shore and observed feral goats that quickly vanished if approached too near. Goats appear totally unsuitably built for the rock climbing at which they excel. These were in many different colours, some completely white. They all had the shaggy culotte legs of Mr Tumnus, and all showed total confidence climbing on the steep wooded rocks.

The wind kept it chilly, despite the sun that now shone to glorify our surroundings. We came close to the shore past Foyers, where there is a small power station. This is a pumped-storage power station. The main building, housing huge turbines in deep pits, is right on the shore of the loch and has a long section of stone embankment extending to several hundred metres, giving a hard edge to the water body. This type of power generation involves raising water levels to a high reservoir during off-peak periods and releasing it later to generate additional power at times of peak demand. This was the first large-scale UK hydro-electric scheme, originally built in 1896. The storage reservoir is 180 metres above Loch Ness and was created by joining two small lochs to form Loch Mohr.

The waves were coming across the loch and hitting the wall of the power station banks at about sixty degrees and deflecting back, causing unusual wave movements. We had come quite close to the building and this wave interference was causing us difficulties. I was expecting at least one of us to tip over. The interference came in very unexpected ways, so when expecting movement from waves in one direction, there might be simultaneous movement from somewhere else. Occasionally we were in the midst of perfect clapotis, where waves occur without movement and the peaks and troughs are occurring at the same spot. Sometimes chaotic wave patterns collided around us, causing a pyramid-shaped wave with a spout of water thrown high from the peak. It was impossible to read. The surface of the water was a swirling choppy maelstrom and we paddled out into the loch as quickly as we could.

Near the banks of the loch just north of the power station is Boleskine House. It is not of special architectural interest but was home to Aleister Crowley between

1899 and 1913. Scotland has given the world many talented mountaineers, and Crowley was accomplished and well known in that field, but notoriety in other aspects of his life had been unusually strange. Crowley became infamous for stories of black magic and satanic ritual, much of it carried out here on the banks of Loch Ness. He referred to himself as 'the Great Beast 666' and the tabloids gave him a memorable title: 'The Wickedest Man in the World'.

We had planned to camp on a small disused pier a mile on from Foyers. We were there by late afternoon, and we established a camp in our usual way. Brunel had regularly featured on our Thames journey, but the Victorian engineer featuring on this journey was Thomas Telford. The little pier, not much more than a small platform of land projecting a few metres into the loch, with solid stone-built moorings and a few oversized rusting bollards, had been built by Telford as part of the grand scheme of his canal thoroughfare.

We sponged out our boats and Mark walked along the shore to where the small River Farigaig empties into the loch. Dave and I stripped off and swam round to where Mark had seated himself on the shore. We made a weak effort to be monster-like as we rounded the promontory and came into Mark's view, Dave in front with crooked arm aloft and me at the back trying to look like a hump. Mark feigned horror. We splashed about in the cold water until Dave swam off in his expert way. And I went to dry off.

The pier is situated at the foot of a heavily wooded part of the loch, so we decided to walk inland to explore.

The vast primeval wilderness of Scots pine, birch, rowan, aspen and juniper that populated most of Scotland from the end of the last ice age is now restricted to thirty-five small remnants across the Highlands. These areas are of great importance, as the Scots pine and other plant life retain an unbroken nine-thousand-year genetic chain. We were now right at the centre of what was the Caledonian Forest.

The rewilding movement has gained pace significantly in Scotland, but the megafauna that inhabited the forest – grey wolves, elk, and wild horses – are unlikely to return. Beaver were reintroduced in parts of Scotland in 2009, and there are controversial suggestions to reintroduce wolves. It is not just the romantic and headline-grabbing factor with wolves and other impressive predators that promote them for reintroduction. The ecosystems that evolved in the Caledonian Forest relied on these predators as a keystone species and effected the whole environment in a top-down trophic cascade, where the top predators control the primary consumer population. Removal of these predators alters the whole food web dynamic. The forest began to diminish once man established there, eliminating predators, introducing sheep, and clearing for agriculture. By the seventeenth century, high densities of sheep, cattle and wild deer were everywhere, and the forest was unable to regenerate.

There are large areas of sparse population in Scotland, which make it a good candidate for restoration of lost habitat. George Monbiot's *Feral*, gives an interesting account, among other rewilding issues, of how the admired grassy hills of Wales are in fact a degraded and barren wasteland with extremely poor biodiversity. The thousands of acres of Scottish hills, lauded for the heather and the spectacular open views, are similarly degraded. Isabella Tree's book, *Wilding*, tells the story of her remarkable endeavour to dramatically improve biodiversity and sustainability at the Knepp Estate in West Sussex, in my own part of the UK, the busy and overcrowded South-East. Rewilding has broad interpretations, but urban man's reconnection with his relationship with the land is all part of this, and is something largely uncontroversial.

There was plenty of daylight remaining as we entered the woods known as Farigaig Forest. We saw red squirrels and signs of deer. We constantly heard woodpeckers drilling. We knew that pine martens were frequent, but we weren't lucky enough to glimpse any.

We followed a section of trail but decided to wander off the path. There were conifers of all ages and mature deciduous trees spread out in between enormous Douglas fir.

The views through clearings towards the loch presented tall stands of blood-red foxgloves among vibrant green bracken with unfurling shooting tips, like a bishop's crook. Butterflies flitted and fluttered. Scots pine bordered the view like a book cover illustration.

The canopy was not so dense that light could not permeate, and angled shafts of light striped all around like animal camouflage. The atmosphere was wet. Moss covered almost everything and gave the uneven ground, landscaped with hummocks, the look of model railway mountains. Mosses are unlike other plants; they are bryophytes, meaning that they lack vascular structures or liquid-conducting tissues, such as xylem and phloem found in trees. Moss has a spongy softness like an expensive fabric. It tempts you to sit on it, but the spongy look is not deceptive; it holds a lot of water. The most widespread moss of the boreal forests is also common here: the aptly named glittering wood-moss. It is like small yellow-green fern growth and was densely upholstering fallen trees and boulders all around. The moss-scape came in colours of reds and greens. The way the light reached parts of the forest floor was like light through water when revealing a submarine landscape of coral on an undersea escarpment. I dug my hand into a carpet of the splendidly named big shaggy-moss, which revealed mites, nematodes, tiny beetles, spiders, and abundant crawling life, active and thriving.

Lichen has its own role in the evolution of the forest. It secretes acids that can dissolve rock, helping to start the process of soil formation, and it decorated exposed rock with tones of rust and cream where the moss had not taken hold. Ferns grew from cracks on the mini canyons of many tiny streams, splashing and mumbling along the forest floor. The air was perfumed heavily with resin, but the musty dank smell of fungus threaded through the trees as a reminder of decay and regeneration. An impressive variety of fungus emerged through the moss with violet, cream, and magenta colours. The fruiting body of a mushroom or toadstool is only a tiny part of the organism; a huge network of mycelium spreads underground throughout the forest. The woodland trees and fungus are all interdependent and live symbiotically in the forest ecosystem. Insects were in constant motion – some not so friendly – ants marched underfoot and biting insects droned above.

Mark was the one the insects liked the most, and unlike Dave and I, he was in shorts. He needed to get back to trousers. The first of the evening's midges bit. Covering up was urgent. We half ran back to our pier and made a frantic race, tearing at dry bags in panic to find clothes to cover any flesh, like unfaithful lovers hearing the cuckold on the stairs.

We were glad to be rid of the midge torture once on the water again in the morning. The low sun gave us a romantic view of Urquhart Castle on the other bank, worthy of the finest tartan-trimmed all-butter shortbread biscuit tin. The wind had changed to push us on from behind.

We again decided to paddle out into the middle of the loch. I told Dave and Mark that I felt at least some uneasiness knowing that the water was so deep and dark below. They did not share this trepidation at all. There is no logic to it, but I understand that, for some, thalassophobia, as it is called, can be a problem that affects their lives in unexpected ways. Loch Ness is the second deepest body of water in the UK and holds more fresh water than all the rivers, lakes and reservoirs in England and Wales combined. It is 230 metres deep at the deepest point. The high peat content of the surrounding soil gives it a murky blackness with very poor underwater visibility.

All the rivers and waterways that we have travelled elicit their own emotional response and the character of each waterway can change as it progresses. The northern end of Loch Ness has an uncomfortable hint of blackness. It has something of the fear of the subconscious. We live our lives on the surface, but on water there is a sense of 'below' that you don't get on land. It is the opposite of the feeling of hope and optimism I felt on the wide, braided lengths of the Vjosa which I later describe. Loch Lochy and Loch Oich gave a similar hint of oppression but offered a cosy intimacy lacking on Loch Ness. The mountains, islands and seascape between Oban and Fort William had been contemplative and induced thought. In Loch Ness, there is a background sense of impending doom. Interior spaces in homes, public buildings, churches or whatever, can give you a sense of happiness, and a space can feel comfortable or even comforting to be present within. They can also feel chilling and unwelcome. Landscapes have a similar subjective effect on us. This end of the loch had 'owlness'. There is something here of the unfathomable bleak emptiness of the barn owl's inert, passionless eye.

A body of water with these characteristics would inevitably collect stories of strange and frightening beasts, but for international fame, few surpass Nessie. There are ancient references to the beast in the sixth century with Saint Columbus saving one of his followers by making the sign of the cross just when he was about to be devoured by the creature. 'Beyond this place there be beasts,' would have been the call at a time when unicorns cast their magic spell and sea monsters and mermaids were to be found here and there. It was the 1933 photograph and subsequent article in *The Inverness Courier* that first gripped international attention. There is no reliable evidence that any kind of monster exists. Steve Feltham arrived on the banks of the loch in 1991 to make a committed vigil to solve the mystery and he has now spent most of his life in this search. Spending your life seeking what is not there is a common theme among mankind, but I doubt that Nessie has everlasting life on offer. We were hoping to find Steve in Dores at the northern end of the loch where he lives in a converted mobile library, but there was no sign of him when we stopped there. I wonder if you can actually wear out a pair of binoculars?

We were approaching the northern end of the loch when we saw our first osprey. It was at high level and appeared directly over us. I have seen osprey before in Scotland but exhibiting speed and purpose. This bird was in no hurry. He was lolling around the clear sky on patrol. I was surprised by the length and narrowness of his M-shaped wings. The males have especially narrow wings.

Both have four distinctive finger-like feathers on their wing tips. He had the look of a red kite but seemed strangely awkward as he cruised along, retaining some grace, like an over-tall adolescent boy.

His progress was of a similar speed to ours. The uneasiness that I had felt at the northern end of Loch Ness was lifting more and more with each gentle beat of his wings. He followed us like this from the end of the loch for three or four miles towards Inverness, where we decided this time to take the river route and leave the canal.

We made our way along the river with a few low-grade rapids, and we decided to shoot two weirs, which we successfully negotiated without incident. There were some very shallow sections, and it was on one of these that we were rewarded with a great sighting of a dipper. We had seen these busy little birds on the River Wye, but not so close. On the Tweed we saw scores of them. The bird is an active plump underwater forager with the round body of a wren, about the size of a sparrow. We were near enough to hear its bright whirring call, and the stubby-winged flight could be heard buzzing at high speed as it flitted between rocks. It has a white bib on its breast that flashes as it continually bobs or dips in and out of the water, from where it presumably gets its name. The bird occasionally disappeared underwater for almost a minute at a time. The dipper is the only passerine that has this ability.

We arrived on the edge of Inverness. Like other towns in Scotland, a symphony of grey, where a campsite, close enough to drag our boats to, gave us the chance of a shower and a clean-up.

We had decided on an evening in the town. We first ate a classic haggis and neep meal at a simple café where we were served with a tall cylinder of moulded mashes presented in the middle of our plates in a small pool of gravy, with one third a stratum of mashed potato, one third orange neeps, all topped with a two-inch layer of haggis. It was hot, welcome, and delicious.

To our surprise, there were a lot of American military out for the evening. RAF Lossiemouth is nearby where the US Navy stations various aircraft. It seems that Britain hasn't yet let go of the Cold War. All seemed to be very young and very polite, even respectful. I found the Americans easier to understand than the locals.

There was more cheering in the bars watching England lose again in the World Cup, this time to Uruguay. We kept our heads down. All made us welcome and showed interest in what we were doing. We may have had a few whiskies.

※

A campsite gave us a better opportunity to dry off and repack our kit before our final leg, which would be seagoing on the east coast. When we were afloat the next day, it was with the warm glow of a hot shower and dry clothes.

The river makes a gentle route through the town towards the harbour. We knew that the harbour and the sea were approaching, and the river gained depth and stronger flow. There was a large-lettered traditional sign-written building on the right, reading 'D. Chisholm & Sons. Funeral Home, established 1875,' This is Dave's name and in view of what was about to happen, I feel lucky it wasn't prophetic. We could see a bridge in front of us and we could feel the current increase. Dave was a little in front and I saw him quite suddenly back-paddle and he called out, 'Hazard, hazard!'

I looked over towards Dave and back at Mark. While distracted, the bow of my kayak slid hard against a large rock that was only just submerged. The current swung the back of the boat around and as I tried to correct the tilt, the back hit another rock and quickly turned the boat over. The water was chest deep, but the riverbed was littered with these partly submerged rocks. The vessel was fully loaded and I was immediately wedged between large rocks, which gave me little chance to roll back upright. I pulled the straps of the spray deck with strange underwater sounds muffled in my ears. The spray deck snapped off, allowing me to crawl out underwater. In that upside-down world, the current felt like a great weight bearing down. I was able to stand and brace myself against one of the taller rocks to avoid being swept with the flow. I had grabbed the side line of the kayak and was safe for now. Dave and Mark had managed to reverse away from the hazard, which was an unexpected weir under the bridge that we had missed on the map. It was low tide and the river crashed down six feet or so over jagged boulders. We had no helmets and no intention of attempting to ride the obstacle. I needed rescuing.

We had plenty of rope and it was only the central channel that presented problems – exactly where I was stuck. Mark threw a line, and I attached my kayak, which was easily pulled ashore. Dave waded out towards me onto a shallow bank about 4 metres away. I could see another rock one pace away. He threw me a line that I used to steady myself as I tried to wade to this second bracing point. I had thought it a good idea to wear warm and heavy-duty plus-two breeks that morning. A bad idea. They filled with water and acted like an underwater sail. I was wearing a buoyancy aid, but I didn't like the idea of being dragged over the weir rocks like a keelhauling. Cool heads prevailed and we were after all in no hurry. I was OK where I had ended up. With the help of the line, I was able to gain enough traction on the riverbed, part me wading, part Dave pulling, to eventually reach Dave's hand, which pulled me onto the shallow bank. I had escaped safely.

Dave has seen difficulties with swimmers at sea and was not flustered by our near miss. Mark deals with danger on a regular basis when on the mountains, but for me riding a bike around Hyde Park Corner is as close as I usually come to real danger. This had been a near miss, but we'd treated it as just another challenge on our way.

We carried the boats around the weir, one by one. There was a small but disused launch ramp on the eastern bank, in front of an industrial estate, where we unpacked our stove and settled with tea to take stock. Everything on the front of my boat had been securely strapped down and the rubber lids of two holds at either end had stayed secure and proved themselves watertight. We looked out over the gushing weir to assess if we could have made it if we hadn't been able to stop. Plenty of white-water kayakers would think little of it, but we had very long boats not designed for that kind of thing, no safety helmets, and no experience of anything so big.

The weather had improved, and I had taken off my drenched clothes, and continued in trunks only. It was shirts-off sunshine as we made our way past large working ships. There were two enormous and very elegant wind turbine blades lying on the dock, white and matt, like whale bones. We had reached the other coast. Mark offered up a hand as if clasping a glass to toast this milestone.

The three of us drew up together in the harbour mouth to offer this toast with a fake clink. Immediately, and to our great delight, a dolphin arched up right next to the three kayaks, less than a metre away. We were open-mouthed with raised eyebrows as we looked at each other. It seemed like a magic charm. It must be good luck. The dolphin followed us out of the harbour.

There is a constriction here where the Beauly Firth to the west meets Rosemarkie Bay to the east, and we knew that the tide was not at a turning point. Dave had taken the precaution of contacting the harbour master to let him know our plans, and that offered some reassurance in case of incident. The cable-stayed Kessock Bridge spans this point from Inverness to the Black Isle peninsula. A headwind had brewed up unexpectedly and the tide was running west to east. We had less than a mile to cross and we set a course accounting for the tidal drift, and it was a fifteen-minute head-down push in close formation.

We stopped at one of the elephantine concrete footings of the bridge and collected a bucket of hairy mussels, white with barnacles, for later that evening.

The north-eastern route along the coast was sheltered and became a pleasant bimble. Another osprey seemed to follow us, as before, unhurried and lazy. Sea birds and sea air changed the character of the day completely. A pleasant iodine tang was in our nostrils and on our tongues. Curlews and oystercatchers called long fluting song into the clear air like a ship's whistle. The seaside rocks of the Black Isle were black with seaweed, and black cormorants sunned themselves on black buoys. I could see turnstones running busily on the shore, and other waders drifted in flocks, landing and taking off incessantly. We paddled past some quiet inlets and explored the tranquil Munlochy Bay.

We made it a short day and landed at the small harbour at Fortrose. There is a short grassy pier on one side, and we asked at the yacht club if we could stay there for the night. It was warm and dry, so we assumed that we wouldn't bother with a tent. We had pulled up the boats and planned to spread our mats out on the soft grass. Dave had used his bivvy bag throughout and had been comfortable enough without a tent – and far enough from Mark and me to avoid snore disturbance.

We cooked up our mussel haul for an early supper and then we walked into the village. We looked around the abandoned cathedral and admired the stained glass in the church. Fortrose is a tiny place to have a cathedral, but like places of strategic worth, on a promontory protecting access to Inverness, it had former importance. We read a little of its history. We made a longer walk into Rosemarkie, an attractive, red stone village. We found a pub called The Anderson, run by an enthusiastic American. We walked into a warm atmosphere with a warm welcome. Every surface was cluttered with all manner of art and curios. They had a vast collection of whisky on offer from all over the world, served with a written note of explanation on each to help the drinker's appreciation. The landlord was also a Belgian beer connoisseur, and the range available was impressive. We stayed till dark and sampled more than we ought to have. We had a long stumble back to the harbour and our boats. We all crashed out happily, but heavy rain came at two in the morning. Dave didn't even wake in his bivvy, but Mark and I, in lightweight sleeping bags only, had to take action. We fumbled around in the kayak hold to find our tent and did our best to erect it as quickly as we could. We slept like wet dogs.

✻

We had little distance to paddle on our last day and planned only a few miles to finish at Rosemarkie.

We set off late and were already approaching the end of the bay. The sun was warm on our backs. We steered a course quite close to the shore to round the short peninsula. Quite unexpectedly, as we approached faster flowing water, the distinctive curve of a bottlenose dolphin slid above the surface of the water, not 2 metres from Dave's kayak. Then another, then more around my boat, then we saw one make a full leap clear of the water near Mark's kayak.

These were large creatures. Similar in size to our kayaks. The sense of wonder being among these silky, joyful mammals was utterly thrilling. The curtain of the pantomime went up.

'He's behind you!' yelled Mark as another dolphin broke the surface behind Dave, only some 50 metres offshore. In no time, there were many of them. The repetitive half-circular gleaming backs of the pack were like a Victorian wave machine at a theatre. They were playing to us. Quite clearly aware of, and interested in, our presence.

There is a narrow channel at the seaward end of Rosemarkie Bay, at Chanonry Point, where it is less than a mile across to Fort George on the opposite shore. There is also a narrow peninsula on the opposite side. It is after this pinch point that the bay opens to the Moray Firth. This is home to Britain's largest population of bottlenose dolphin. The feature produces faster water when the tide is in full turn and fish are both forced into this bottleneck and attracted to the flow. It becomes a place for the dolphin to play and to feed. We were right in the fray. We paddled as slowly as we could and hung around enjoying the spectacle, before heading down the northern side, which is a long stretch of clean sand.

We booked into a campsite there for our last night and spent the afternoon at a beach nestled into the crook of the bay in a hollow at the foot of inland hills. We swam and relaxed and took stock of what we had completed.

We went back to The Anderson for the evening, and we presented our American friend with the figurehead of Mark's kayak, the sheep's skull, which we had inscribed in black marker with the words: 'Oban to Fortrose. Kayak 2014. Mark. Dave. Nick,' He placed this on the reception counter – where it stayed for years.

The campsite warden had used a spray can to paint out the demarcation of our pitch on the grass. A great spot overlooking the beach with a westward view over the Moray Firth. In the morning, he came on his patrol around the campers and stood in front of us with his hands on his hips as we were packing our bags. 'Who's the clever one then?' he asked. We were puzzled. 'Come on, who was it? Which one of you lot couldn't even put their tent up?' He hadn't finished. 'I don't put them marks on the grass for nothing. One of you was right out of line, well outside your pitch'.

We knew then what he was policing. I rested my finger casually on my top lip and pointed with a flat hand in a thinly disguised Hitler impression, and said, 'Ah, over there. Yes, Dave was over the line, and he only uses a bivvy,' Dave and Mark had to look elsewhere. I controlled myself long enough as he shook his head and walked off. We annoyed him again later by drying our shoes in his pound-a-go clothes drier.

Our kayaks were collected, and we had a short taxi trip to Inverness Airport. We were all back at my house to go our separate ways by mid-afternoon, our heads full of happy memories. We always meet shortly after each journey for a debriefing to assess what we had achieved and enjoyed, and we would then start planning our next journey.

CHAPTER 5
THE VJOSA

Wealth squanders riches that poverty preserves

The vast ring of forest and wetland which is the Taiga, the world's largest biome, circles the northern dome of the globe like a monk's tonsure. This vast green carbon-capturing resource and its adjoining oceans are teeming with life. It is also the last extensive domain of wild, unrestrained rivers.

Untamed but of little fame, there is the mighty Amur-Heilong in both China and Russia; Siberia has both the huge Nizhnyaya Tunguska and the Aldan rivers. More familiar to us in the west is the Mackenzie and the Peace River in Canada and the Yukon in Alaska.

These rivers of the Taiga, along with countless smaller ones, traverse many thousands of miles through sparsely populated forest and tundra, which is still ruled by bears, wolves, tigers, and other majestic apex predators.

The closest we had been to this domain of wild rivers was when we kayaked between two tectonic plates in Scotland. This had been dabbling on the fringes of the Taiga. We wanted to find an accessible waterway that retained this spirit.

All the continents have a few impressive water courses, but in most of Europe, thousands of years of farming, fishing, and total dominance by man, has shifted the physical geography of the landscape and skewed the natural order of flora and fauna. Rivers are tamed. A very few, precious rivers in Europe do still run their natural untampered course through the landscape.

The vast and mighty rivers of the Taiga, with herds of caribou and grisly predators, may see the River Rats one day, but for now we would settle on our own more modest level of epic, and take on the Vjosa of Albania. It is the last large-scale free-flowing river in Europe. Its course is unhampered by man's interference. Its early parts are fast flowing and remote, and wind through sculpted rocks in the Greek then the Albanian mountains. The central section is a broad 2-km-wide braided entanglement of streams, with scores of different channels that snake through a shifting gravelly bed. It runs through gorges and steep wooded banks, but also, as the river slows and deepens, through flat plains and well-tilled farmland where fisherfolk dip nets into the current all day long. The final length leads a straight channel to the cobalt Dalmatian Sea.

The catchment area of the Vjosa basin is largely made up of forest and grassland. It is a wild place.

RIVER
SEPTEMBER
162 KM
KASHISHT
21-Km day
PORO
FITORE
40-Km day
30-Km day
25-Km day
SELENICE
St. Mary's Monastery
9-Km day
9-Km day
REX-HEPAJ
H ZVËRNEC
VLORË
FINISH
CAMP
HOTEL
Dave Chisholm FRGS
St Mary's
Strait of Otranto
OOOFF!
Bunker
10
20
30
KILOMETRES
ALB

VJOSA
8TH-16TH 2017
SLO
HR
RO
BH
SRB
I
RKS
BG
MNE
Adriatic Sea
AL
NMK
Ionian Sea
GR
TR
Mediterranean Sea
TORTOISE
N
E
W
S
KALIVAC
QESARAT
TEPLENË
28-km day
Monastery
START
River Drino
River Vjosa
H
ANIA
GJIROKASTËR

We had settled on kayaking this river, having read about a group of canoeists calling themselves the Balkan River Defence, whose campaign to save the Vjosa was titled 'Save the Blue Heart of Europe'. Turkish hydropower developers had been granted access to test sites on the river to build huge dams. This could be our own *Deliverance*, with or without duelling banjos. No doubt that Dave would want to be Burt Reynolds.

Mark had carried out the geographical research on the expedition and Dave had largely sought out local help with kayak hire and advice on logistical detail in Albania. I had organised transport, accommodation, and a few other travel essentials.

We set off early one September morning from Gatwick on a return ticket to Corfu. On arrival, we travelled to Corfu port and boarded the open-topped, thirty-minute ferry to Saranda in Albania. We were immediately submerged in the intoxicating heat and buzz of the adventure. We found a taxi to take us, with our minimal baggage, the 60 kilometres to Gjirokaster. The town has enough significance to be granted UNESCO World Heritage status.

We had booked a room for the three of us to share in an old stone building. By mid-afternoon, we had checked in and headed straight out into the sunshine, having left a little time to explore the well-preserved Ottoman Old Town. Gjirokaster is built strategically on the edge of a sweeping valley in the Gjere Mountains. It is known as the 'Stone City'. Cobblestone streets and old white stone buildings with oversized stone roof tiles give the feeling that it grew from the bedrock of the mountain.

There are tourist shops and a holiday feel to the place. We scampered around the huge fortress at the apex of the town and, as dusk fell, settled for drinks and supper on a broad terrace with a spectacular evening view over the expansive verdant valley below.

There were scores of lesser kestrels gracefully swooping the heights in front of us, catching airborne insects, much like oversized swifts with crossbow wings and dare-devil speed. A horizontal raft of billowing cloud, highlighted by the very last disc of the dying sun, lingered across the high ground on one side of the valley in the ever-dwindling light.

We chatted excitedly under the outside table lamp, poring over the maps and program details spread out in front of us with cold beer in hand.

Back in our lodgings, the beds seemed to be built like children's bunkbeds in the small room, one on top of a wardrobe and the other two at different floor levels. Mark lobbed a pillow from his high perch and a rolled-up sleeping bag was returned at high speed. Eventually Zebedee said, 'Time for bed,' This would be our last night in a bed for some time.

※

In the morning, we were met as arranged by a courteous man in his twenties, who had travelled all the way from Tirana to meet us. He owned an Outward Bound school and had agreed to rent us three kayaks. He took us the short journey from where, at this time of year, the river is just deep enough to navigate.

There was a roadside stall where we sorted out the paperwork over tiny cups of strong *kafe Turke*. The disorganised shelves were packed, and you could buy anything you might want here – just so long as it was honey. There were many gallons of it, stored in all manner of stone, glass, or plastic receptacles. Albanian honey is the best and most varied you can find.

The spot was near a well-known spring. A gushing but tiny waterfall noisily roared through the middle of the balcony where we sat. Everything seemed fresh and clean; even the air was washed by the spray.

We unloaded the craft and carried them down to the water's edge. We packed our kit in the normal way in the two holds each end of each kayak. In no time we were gliding effortlessly on the shallow white water. The magic of the first buoyancy made us feel light and uplifted, a feeling all kayakers understand. We were soon in a deeper channel with the magnificent Vjosa ahead.

Our start was full of surprise at sights that would later become commonplace. Goat herders with dogs, the enormous broad views, the distinctive bleached white stones on the river's edge.

The river quickly broadened. The pace of the flow increased, especially on the outside of the meander bends, where the water deepens.

The colour and tone of the water was ever changing, but for the first thirty miles always retained a distinctive milky quality. Later, as the soil became more fertile, the gravel became less ubiquitous and the white boulders along the banks disappeared; the water also gained a yellow ochre tinge with blackish depths.

The scent of the river altered gradually in the same way. The gravelly braided sections had a vigorous mineral scent. Other sections had the sweet sharp scent of wet grass after summer rain. Later, the overall impression was more earthy, faintly manure-like. The different woodland added another dimension to this experience. White willow and white poplar dominated the broader parts. In some sections, tamarisk and scrub gave way to oriental plane and black locust; in others, mixed oak and pine woods lent a resinous tinge to the air.

After a speedy five or six miles, we had reached Tepelenë. We paddled past our first bridge. It was a kind of suspension footbridge. One side anchored into a stone cliff and on the other side, on the inside of the bend, it was held aloft by large war relic-like concrete columns, built on an older stone foundation. We then passed under a heavy cable, the metallic strands fractured and frayed with rust, that was strung across the river. We decided to pull up here to investigate.

The Tepelenë side was close to the town, but where we had hauled our boats onto the stones, beautifully rounded by river attrition, there was no road, no path, just scrubby bush. Who would have used this crossing?

There was a rusty steel cage suspended from the thick wire, creaking in the breeze. This was evidence of some historic cable car form of transport over the river. The crossing seemed to connect to nowhere. A broken-down concrete block shack at the extreme end, where the cable was anchored into the rock, suggested that it had once been a motorised system.

The cable was only 2 or 3 metres above the water, so we were aware that river craft were not expected this far upriver.

Tepelenë, a small ancient town of fewer than ten thousand, had once been the seat of power of a famous individual who became known as Ali Pasha, the 'Lion of Yanina', a servant of the declining Ottoman Empire in the early nineteenth century. He had been a ruthless and successful brigand, whose strategy was to ostensibly join with the Ottoman sultan, but truly only to serve his own ambition. Byron has a well-known association with Albania, and he visited Ali Pasha here in 1809. The town has place names and monuments to both people.

Byron had also visited Gjirokaster and wrote to his mother that Albania was 'a country of the most scenic beauty,' The beauty is certainly still evident. Byron was taken by the impossibly extravagant gilt thread and crimson velvet of the courtly dress. The famous portrait of Byron, now in the National Gallery, by Thomas Phillips, shows Byron in Albanian costume. This extravagance is certainly not still evident.

Edward Lear travelled the Balkans, spending much time in Albania, writing a journal and painting the landscape. He too had visited Gjirokaster and Tepelenë.

'There were three men in their kayaks' and a string of weak limericks, mainly based on Vjosa rhyming with tosser, were attempted as we climbed into our cockpits and set off for our first afternoon afloat. Clouds started to gather, changing the temperature and blurring the vistas for a while. Our spirits were high. We caught each other smiling gratuitously. Life was good. We're doing this thing!

We continued for a few hours with just one stop on the slow-moving side of a meander for a welcome brew. By half past six in the evening, we had reached our planned distance target for the day, so we looked out for a good bivvy spot to camp.

We had by now entered the beginnings of one of the broad braided lengths of the river. The plain around us was close to a mile wide. We chose a raised bank of heavy shingle with copious bundles of brush, trees, and debris that would make a steady fire.

Mark immediately set about preparing water from the river with our filter. We knew the routine that had evolved between us for settling down, so a small fire was lit and the camp was set up efficiently. The kayaks were now secure and high on the shingle. The spray skirts were hung out to dry like animal hides curing on the bony white driftwood.

We had expected only good weather and we had decided not to bring a tent. We would bivvy down under the stars. There are still wolves, lynx, and bears in the mountains of Albania. They are rare and, thankfully, managed, but we tried hard to spook each other as dusk descended.

I was on cooking duty that evening. Today was the tenth anniversary of our first Thames trip. Touchingly, Mark brought out three little glasses, painted with Thames themes. He also had a tiny greeting card for us both. The incongruity of all this made it all the more enjoyable. Our simple evening meal was eaten with local red wine poured from a plastic bottle into our souvenir glasses. We chatted away, congratulating ourselves on a fabulous first day and enjoying memories from the Thames.

It was calm. We had each dug a kind of nest in the sandy stones for our bivvy bags. The night sky was clear and sparkled with stars far brighter than we are used to at home. I felt relief and satisfaction, with a measure of wonder and anticipation. The mesmerising night chorus of insects, Dave's snoring, and the lullaby of the Vjosa, led me happily to a deep sleep.

⁕

We awoke to climbing temperatures and blazing sun that had already burnt its rays through the haze while still low on the eastern horizon. A crescent moon was clear on the western side. I made an early brew and fried a few eggs with bacon, stuffed them between pillowy white bread rolls, and handed them round. After a solitary morning stroll over a few gravel banks with the trowel, always a much-discussed piece of kit, we packed up carefully and checked our maps.

RIVER RATTING

We knew from Mark's research that rapids lay ahead. There seemed to have been little interest from other kayakers in paddling this section of the river, so there was no information on the internet. High up stream, where there is serious white water in the wetter times of year, skilled slalom sportspeople had mapped and catalogued what to expect. We largely relied on Google satellite.

We set off cheerfully. The first floating of the day always brings a sense of lightness, and at this spot, it felt joyful. The current was fair, and the first ten miles were spent absorbing the beauty of the broad landscape and deciding on which route to take of the many independent courses the river was now offering. The river here was several hundred metres across. At times, it sprawled along the gravel like the many yarns and fibres of an untwisting rope. At these areas we occasionally missed the deeper channel and had to climb out of our kayaks and walk in the gushing shallows. It became a source of superiority if one of us managed to avoid this when the others were walking. 'You two haven't quite got this right yet. Amateurs, the pair of you,' crowed Mark gleefully.

The deep banks of stones and boulders spread throughout the plain, all smooth and pastel shades, like so many sugared almonds, had an average size between that of a mango and a melon. Their topography, as much a flailing twine as the gullies and streams between them, disclosed the true nature of the river. Geologists call this a juvenile river. The stones illustrate a high-energy environment. Solid matter is suspended in the water and as the energy diminishes, so the deposited grain size diminishes. Further downstream, the grain size becomes apples and pears, then gooseberries down to blackcurrants until any fruit analogy turns to sand. At least when wet the colour palette of the stony jewels retains its fruit-like colour palette.

By midday we were approaching a gorge. The current became strong on the bends, but we felt no need to halt, so we enjoyed the ride as grade two rapids hurried us along to the towering yellow walls of the gorge. Once inside, the sound quality changed dramatically to echo. The sun disappeared. The temperature dropped. We were passing through a dominion of trepidation.

It took just ten minutes to weave our way through the gorge where the rapids ended, but deep fast-flowing water took over. Some of the sharper twists in the river were a challenge in our long kayaks. The tighter the bend, the faster the flow.

Once safely through, we stopped on the shallow slope of an inside bend to gather our thoughts. We felt relieved to be downstream of these rapids and the gorge, all intact, with no capsize or kayak roll attempt required. We had very loosely laid plans of where to arrive that day and we decided to stick to that plan, which would mean a 30-kilometer stint overall.

CHAPTER 5 — THE VJOSA

The second part of the day was much of the same riverscape. We saw an area, shortly after the gorge, where it appeared that some of the testing had been carried out for the building of a dam. The rocky banks had been carved by giant machinery into flat ledges and square-edged banks. We knew that protests concerning hydro plants were in full force, but big money was at stake. Clever argument could be made in favour of sourcing energy at home. Some believed these hydro ventures to be a 'green' option. Politicians in Albania, like everywhere else, are not exempt from corruption. The dams could be built and this special river with its unique environmental catchments, and its annually altering flood plains, would be lost forever.

We stopped mid-afternoon to rest on a wooded embankment and I tackled up my small rod and reel and tried spinning for whatever might bite. Ironically, I caught nothing, but later that afternoon a six-inch fish, which I later identified as an asp, jumped onto Mark's spray deck as he rode some low-grade rapids.

Mark was so pleased with his fish that he paddled hard to come up to Dave and me to show and tell of his treasure. It would likely grow to a fair size in recounting later: the monster that leapt onto his boat in dangerous rapids, the enormous size almost sinking him.

Nearly all the asp's riverine habitat in the Balkan region is threatened by large-scale hydropower development. Up to fifty schemes on the Danube, Sava, Drava, and Mur rivers are planned. The 'Save The Blue Heart' campaign points out that this would drive riverine populations of this fish species in the region to extinction.

It had been these campaigners who cared very much for the Vjosa that had first attracted us to this river. I have tracked the progress of the campaigns against the hydro development over the years that followed our visit, and they have had at least some apparent success.

We paddled on, stopping to try to chat to a shepherd on the riverbank who was riding a small donkey. He wanted none of it and tried to ignore us. We didn't persevere. If you come upon people in a remote place, it seems a bit odd to encounter behaviour like this. I told Dave to stop frightening the locals by being so friendly. The other highlight of the afternoon was spotting our first white stork on the plain by the river. A beautiful upright bird, with an enquiring tilting stance: a favourite of European fables and tales.

We continued until we knew that the village of Pacem was walking distance from the river. We found a high bank with a kind of beach in front to halt for the day and make camp.

As usual, we hauled the craft some distance from the water, arranging them in formation. We dried off and went through our routine. We could see that a bridge over the river was only a short walk ahead, and a small road led to the village. We made a weak attempt to make our brightly coloured kayaks less visible, then set off on foot, hoping to find somewhere to eat.

It was a deep-cut rocky path to the road, which was a gravel track where a simple concrete bridge spanned the river. We weren't sure who would use such a bridge. Farm machinery here seemed often to be very basic, but no doubt heavy. We turned north, away from the river, and some habitation became visible. We passed several simple concrete houses. A few chickens and children were playing noisily.

There were fields of vegetables and sweet corn in domestic-sized blocks. We saw a large tortoise, slowly making its way across the road in the dust. There was evidence of small-scale gravel mining works in the distance. There were also a few small domed haystacks, built up in the tiny fields by hand and pitchfork, in the traditional manner.

Peering over a scruffy concrete block wall, behind an extremely orderly vegetable garden, with tidy frames for beans and carefully hoed rows of beet and a variety of tomatoes, we could see a broad middle-aged woman, with a tightly tied headscarf over her head. She was wielding a long stick. The stick was quite gently lifted up and brought down calmly while she called a repetitive 'aye aye' kind of chant. It took us a while to see that she was herding fat black turkeys, gobbling and clucking contentedly.

Some of the children had run ahead. We didn't know what to expect in the village, but after twenty minutes or so, we had arrived at a collection of a few houses, some with gardens and cars and some with scruffy yards and tractors.

The children had warned the local bar of our impending arrival and we were heartily welcomed. No English was spoken, but the menu was illustrated with gaudy photographs, and we sat outside under a rush umbrella to order beer and food. There was a selection of concrete tanks behind the bar. It was from these vessels that the cook fished out our trout. He brought them to us, grilled, crispy, and unimaginably delicious, served with fat chips and huge slices of beefsteak tomatoes. I made a fuss about the tomatoes; flavour doesn't exist like that at home.

We enjoyed this bit of civilisation, made more special by being ridiculously cheap. Sated on food and beer and now well after nightfall, we asked the bar owner, in sign language, if he could run us in his car to the bridge. He kindly obliged. He dropped us at the bridge with much generous gesticulation from us and we picked our way slowly back to our boats.

We stumbled about sorting out night kit, then bedded down happily on the grassy bank. Moonlit husks of slender grasses swayed over us in the night breeze. We drifted off to a distant howling that we were sure must be hungry wolves.

⁂

The morning saw us bathing in the clean outer streams of the main flow. We were not going to make an early start today. Mark made a big effort by cooking us excellent pancakes on the tiny stove.

Eventually we were ready.

We took plenty of time for this section. It was deeper and slower moving. The river's entanglement of braided channels was beginning to lessen and a defined deeper stream became prominent. We continued, chatting across the water to each other, until we felt that it was time for a break around midday.

We were low on some supplies, so we ran into one of the banks where we had seen evidence of a road. It was hot. I felt sleepy, so I put up Mark's umbrella as a parasol and lay down for a snooze in the shade. Dave and Mark tied their shirts around their waists and started to walk up a hill along a road where the map appeared to show a few houses. We were hoping for a shop. The boys found an ancient house amongst a few other ramshackle buildings, a part of which passed as a shop. They returned with a few essentials, giddy from having been unable to refuse an offering of local raki from the generous old shopkeeper.

Before crouching back into our kayaks again, we stood together looking at the dramatic scene around us. The landscapes around the Vjosa are like uplifting music. Great curves of graceful slopes, flat plains, and the fluid rhythmic detail of the river's course where it flows in many channels, plays its own symphony with movements of contrast and harmony.

We stood on the washed gravel, watching as the clouds marched with elongated shadows over the escarpment in the distance to the east of the river. On the western side, there were darker, swirling signs of weight in the sky. The view around us was spiritually moving. With the onward progress of our journey now fully underway and the unknown further downriver, the moment had reverence. There was camaraderie, hope, optimism, wonder.

It was so calm and warm, we would never have imagined that later in the afternoon, the western sky would sweep away the calm to the east and we would be challenged by our first and only torrential downpour.

We paddled on for a few hours, the mountainous terrain becoming subdued. The valley floor widened to many miles. The character of the water remained with the same milky freshness. Plenty of fast shallows. The wind was increasing. The river deepened into a dependable channel.

Billowing clouds of sand started racing across the valley, gusting in waves. The grit blasted our faces. Black twisting clouds appeared. The wind became very strong. Paddling against this was frustrating, like eating soup with a fork. Suddenly the rain came. This gave respite from the sand, but the air, heavy with water, whipped up like a sea storm. We had to stop immediately. We pulled up where we could, with the lashing sting of the rain on our arms and heads.

Once the kayaks were safe, we grabbed what we could to cover ourselves, and ran for cover in a willow thicket. We were mindful and worried that such a downpour could flood the river, so we kept a close eye on the water level in case we had to refloat in a hurry.

I was best equipped, with a completely waterproof cape with a hood. I had a great smirk watching Dave and Mark take on the bedraggled appearance of wet dogs while I remained as dry as a Bond martini.

It was a peculiar atmosphere among the willows – like a children's play camp. We talked together in this strangely comfortable place, not knowing if this would be ten minutes or ten hours. The conversation was earnest and intimate. Not so much of the fun and the profane.

The rain was thankfully brief. We were on our way with little wind within forty minutes. It was here that we saw the only vessel we would see on the entire river. Beating away from us was a strange sight, which, at first, was a mystery. What came into focus as we neared the object was a large vehicle inner tube, with two occupants paddling furiously with four stubby single oars, one in each hand. They clearly wore workman-type clothing with the sort of waterproof dungarees you might see on a fishing trawler. There must be a high degree of skill to keep this latter-day coracle in a straight line. They must be fishing, but we couldn't work out how.

This extract from Mark's diary, written later that afternoon, about meeting this unusual-looking vessel illustrates an enlightening point about vulnerability and flight:

We'd had a long day in wind and rain. We now needed to find somewhere to camp. Nowhere was looking suitable. This was not helped by the fast current we found ourselves in and the marshy land along both sides. I was at the back of the group and noticed a tributary had joined us. I paused to look a little longer by back-paddling, as this could possibly provide a site to camp. I needed to check it out closer. Nick and Dave were quickly out of hearing, so I simply got on with checking it. If it was no good, I'd catch them up. If it was suitable, I'd race after them and drag them back! We were running out of options. The current was against me, but by keeping close to the bank, I could make headway until I got into the slower waters of the tributary. It was looking promising. Yes, the far bank had a wide embankment on it, so I paddled across and got out on to the land to investigate further. I climbed up the bank to see if anything unwanted, like houses or farm dogs, was present and to see if there was dry level ground for us three on the top of the embankment. We like to go unnoticed if possible, thereby creating less attention. This is one advantage to sleeping in bivouacking bags rather than tents; their shape doesn't catch the eye like an angular tent. It was good on all counts. I just needed to catch the others up and share the news. With luck, they would have noticed my absence and not travelled too far.

And then I saw it. A large black tractor inner tube pulled tight in the middle with coils of old string to form a rudimentary oval rubber dingy. In the front half, kneeling, was an older, unshaved man in dungarees, staring at me. He didn't look friendly. Behind sat a younger man, also looking my way. They were coming down the tributary straight towards my shiny boat! I didn't feel at all safe being cut off from my kayak. I suddenly realised that I was alone, surrounded by unknown marshland, and even my paddling mates didn't know where I was. This, coupled with this unsavoury pair cutting off my retreat, made me feel vulnerable. I ran towards my boat. When halfway there, I could see I was going to get there first. Relief. I still didn't feel happy or safe until I was afloat. Maybe that's how a seal feels when hauled up on a falling tide with people approaching. I must have been long enough into the trip to feel more confident of myself on the water than on land, because once I had pushed off from the side, the pair no longer felt like a threat. I could outmanoeuvre them if need be. I relaxed and said, 'Hello, where am I?' They were not a threat, just coarsely dressed fishermen, who quickly passed down the river. My situation had let my imagination get the better of me.

We hadn't caught up with this pair before we drew up alongside the first riverside village that we had come across. The surrounding banks by now were steep and high in places. The flood plain areas must be behind us.

The village, sadly, seemed to dump a fair amount of plastic waste straight down a muddy chute directly into the river. We had seen a large quantity of plastic litter and debris throughout our trip.

We couldn't find a good place to land, so we tied up to some trees whose root systems were holding off erosion from the high banks with the village above. We were able to scramble up the bank to the settlement. This was Kashishtë.

The sun had thankfully returned, but the ground was saturated. We walked along a track towards the concrete houses. It was like a medieval scene. Rickety enclosures held back skinny cattle. There were goats bleating, chickens clucking contentedly, and a small white donkey staring us down. It was lightly wooded and pleasant with the sun's dappled shade playing at our feet.

After a hundred metres, we were in the village proper. A poverty-stricken ensemble of decay and make-do. The housing, often looking just a few decades old, was largely single storey, the roads were gravel and mud, but laid out in a modern-looking planned grid. There were signs of pride in appearance at a few of the properties with decorative vines over breeze-block walls and well-tended vegetable gardens.

We found the shop. One of the few two-storey buildings in sight. Plain and institutional-looking, the village bar was attached. We entered and were greeted with great smiles from a rotund middle-aged lady with a solid strength to her stance and glance. We would have been unusual visitors. She knew in advance that we were approaching and we found out later that she had already summoned the schoolteacher to translate.

The teacher arrived. She was sophisticated by comparison with our shopkeeper. She was very young, charming in a mildly bashful way, and spoke good English. The contents of the shop were more like a mini warehouse. Large cases of bottled drinking water, detergent, and the like. We collected vegetables, wine, and a few other supplies, then we were directed to an outside terrace where we were served coffee.

We were surprised to see a new black Mercedes draw up on the muddy street outside the bar. Two large men, possibly only in their twenties, emerged. They were, bizarrely, in white shirts and black suits, which were stretched tightly over their thick knees and broad backs. They sat at the table next to us. We tried to communicate, but they were aloof and cocky, slightly threatening. Their large hands were ogre-like holding the tiny coffee cups. It would be a slur to mention criminality, but it was so incongruous; it was like a scene from a Quentin Tarantino film. Were we about to become the victims in some vicious murder scene? 'We've seen nothing – definitely not fields of cannabis,' I wanted to tell them.

CHAPTER 5   THE VJOSA

In Holland, where marijuana can be legally bought in coffee shops, Albanian is considered a byword for quality. There are thousands of acres of marijuana cultivation in Albania and the unofficial policy is to leave the heavily armed farmers alone.

We made our way back to the river. As we walked past the school, we thanked the teacher across the playground. It had been school break time – perhaps they have a very long lunch – but it was now late afternoon, and the school children were returning to their school. I have earlier commented on the immaculately clean shirts and blazers on the children as they emerged from tatty dwellings into muddy streets, comparing them to the perfectly dressed kingfishers on the Thames as they somehow stayed clean, excavating their nest burrows.

✼

Once back on the river, we passed our second group of fisherfolk. They were a pair of young men wading into quite deep and fast water, adjusting their fish trap.

We paddled on for some time and, as detailed in Mark's account, Dave and I had gained some ground, leaving Mark, without our awareness, to become spooked by the pair in the inner tube. The makeshift craft, like a giant busy beetle, appeared in front of us again, followed closely by Mark. We oared past them, exchanging what was understood to be a greeting.

The river had changed. There was human activity. We paddled on until it was nearly dark. The gravel was replaced by muddy banks. We decided to pitch up on a small concrete groyne. We made a simple pasta meal and sat around discussing what to expect the following day.

It was by now dark. We heard a horse quite close by. We knew it was being ridden because we could also hear a lone voice singing to himself. The voice was rough, out of tune, and panting with the gait of his horse.

To avoid startling the lone rider, we talked deliberately loudly. He became silent and the trot slowed to a walk. We stood up as he approached. He had a rifle laid across his lap. His legs trailed well below the sides of his small horse and nearly scraped the ground. We greeted him in English. He answered with a long monotone sentence in Albanian. Not too friendly. We all kept a close eye on the rifle. Armed men on horseback were something that we were not expecting. Was his talk a challenge? Was he instructing us on some required action? Why would he have a gun? The prickle of fear was not far away. The fight or flight response gurgled in my chest. *There are three of us and one of him*, I thought. Dave gave him a long answer in English with plenty of hand movements, portraying a submissive but friendly attitude. We all smiled uneasily. He couldn't understand us any more than we could understand him. There was a silence of about ten seconds, then he seemed to change and tossed his head back, the strange language became more animated, and his features were distinctly more friendly.

He sounded drunk, but not threatening. I would have preferred to see his hand off the rifle, but he probably also felt a little threatened. Without warning, he marched on into the distance, no longer singing. Watching him from behind, with his substantial frame bouncing up and down owing to the uncomfortable trot of his pony, he appeared more bandit than Clint Eastwood.

We looked at each other with a kind of post-traumatic grin, but we reasoned away any trepidation and thoughts of a returning band of cut-throats. It was an hour or so before we could settle properly. As usual, I was the first to lie down for sleep, this time on mossy concrete. I listened to the others talking the usual nonsense until sleep overtook.

Surprisingly, Albania has a gun culture that is (by gun death count) twice as deadly as the trigger-happy United States. In 1997, when Albania was on the brink of civil war, and a pyramid scheme that had drawn in most of the population collapsed, half of the country's GDP disappeared overnight. It is thought that during the lawless street fighting and looting that followed, up to a million guns were seized from the country's bountiful arms depots.

Rural Albanians, after communism, sometimes reverted to an old custom known as the Kanun. This is an ancient, violent tradition rooted in blood feuds between families. Settling their differences at gunpoint became commonplace. There was recently in Albania a Committee of Nationwide Reconciliation. They estimate that more than 12,000 people have died since 1991 in Albania's blood feuds. There have been UN-backed gun amnesty initiatives, but mopping up such a huge number of weapons, often in remote areas, is an impossible task.

※

The morning was a fine one. It was shirts off before the fire of the midday heat made cover necessary. Mark is fair, Dave is dark and I'm very dark, so our protection needs are in that diminishing order. On the main bank, behind our pier dormitory, trunks and vests had been laid over stout dead vegetation, some of which had toppled over. If there is a shortage of proper bushes, trees and so on, it becomes an art to know what grass or crackly old dried hogweed will support which piece of equipment. A soggy spray deck is a heavy object.

While we brewed our tea and tucked into a fry-up, the sun dried everything off before the day's watery onslaught. Rested, we set off with gleeful anticipation of the day.

The river by now was taking on new character. It was as if its untidy behaviour and wild youth was maturing. There was a single purposeful channel now. It was deeper and altogether more even, with series after series of S-bend meanders.

After a few miles, we were again alongside our beetling inner tube friends. We were greeted by great smiles of nodding recognition. Mark had a view on how they had been fishing – but we were never sure. They may have been working as a team because we soon were padding up to another kind of fishing trap. There was a series of posts driven into the riverbed, clearly forming a 50-metre length of V-shaped trap, culminating in catch nets.

Three men in baseball caps and vests, with lean muscular arms, possibly all called Bruce Willis, were heaving away, waist deep, at an unidentifiable task next to the trap. As the beetle approached, the frantic limbs rested, and as they floated alongside the fisherman, the tone and manner of their fleeting conversation appeared to portray collusion. Dave, the one of us three who tries best to communicate with everyone, tried to ask about their catch. Body language is restricted in a kayak and the response was smiles and incomprehensible words. They were quickly beyond the fishermen, and we were quickly beyond the inner tube that Mark had now dubbed 'the dung beetle'.

As the morning disappeared, the river continued to look more like a watercourse of some activity. We saw a few riverside reed-thatched huts, some with a small boat alongside. The adjacent land was largely farmed and presumably irrigated by the Vjosa. Cereal crops were evident.

The heat was becoming overpowering. Mark erected his umbrella as a parasol with a series of sticks and twine to support it in the wind. Professor Pat Pending, as Dave liked to call him, also used his contraption to capture the wind if it was the correct direction to sail him forward to ease the burden on his tired arms.

We each had our own headwear to keep off the sun. I had a traditional canvas floppy cricket-type hat, Dave kept to a baseball cap, and Mark sported a legionnaire-type hat with ear flaps and a drop behind for neck protection. In Gjirokaster, Mark, to our disappointment, had failed to purchase what we called his 'knob hat'. That might be a cultural insult because the elongated felt fez is part of Albanian national dress. With Mark's stature and inane expression, 'knob' is a fitting title.

※

By early afternoon, we had reached Fitore. There was a heavyweight concrete road bridge and a rail bridge, each with an aged patina of rust stains and white dust. There were scores of fishing rods, all in continuous motion, nodding up and down with vibrating tips as an empty hook or small fish was reeled in. This was habitation proper. There was an urban ambience to the place.

We pulled up against some concrete footings of the bridge and hauled the boats onto the grass. We could see a café up the slope to the road, a hundred metres away. Kids were playing football on a flat area nearby. We were unsure about leaving our kayaks unattended. A tattily dressed gaunt old man, with strong white stubble, smoking a cigarette, came to chat. Although he had a tiny bit more English than Dave had Albanian, they were able to communicate enough so that we felt confident to leave him guarding our kayaks for an undisclosed consideration while we went up to eat at the café.

It was a modern establishment with glass sliding doors and air conditioning. We were not sure if we would be welcome in wet shirts and scruffy looks. As usual, we were, in the event, made very welcome and we enjoyed refreshing beer and plenty of rewarding local food. Once onto coffee, it was a strain to motivate ourselves to make our way back to the boats.

Immediately outside on a road that wouldn't look out of place in a British suburb, as clean expensive cars motored past, several horse-drawn vehicles moved along at a more sedate pace. These reminded me of the gypsy traps we have in the Kentish countryside. They had the kind of make-do technology that was becoming familiar. The wheels were car wheels, and the shafts of the carts were no-nonsense aluminium tubing. The beasts of burden were sadly in a sorry state of health. The juxtaposition of these things was startling.

We offered our guard a small sum, but to our surprise he asked for more. We looked at each other and our lower lips projected as our hands were exhibited palm upwards in a quizzical conciliatory gesture. We had misjudged somewhat. We gave him double, which was still very little.

On our way again, with a post-prandial laziness sapping our strength in the fierce heat, we decided to look out for an early camp. The small town disappeared, and fertile farmland took over on both banks.

We found a likely spot of scrub and sand on a raised bank a few miles on, and set up camp. We lay back in the moderating heat and gazed into the azure sky. Squinting into the haze, at a great height, we saw a group of large-winged birds in squadron formation. I recognised them as cranes. I have seen European cranes very high in the sky before, when I lived in South-West France. They were a sight that local people looked out for as a seasonal marker to confirm that the world was still safely and predictably turning on its axis. These broad-winged birds, in their familiar phalanx, looked very much like those cranes. They may have been another genus but were too large to be white stork. Several crane species and white stork do migrate over this country at this time of year. Those in France would be migrating to Spain for the winter. This stately company would be heading to North Africa.

Bird migration is a thoroughly researched topic. Many thousands of bird species have their different migration habits. Each one is astonishing. There are also many techniques of migration. Some birds set off in flocks, some individually. Some fly at night and some during daylight. Some feed in the air, others land to feed. Some travel many thousands of miles, and others only a few hundred. Migration patterns have evolved over thousands of years. The most startling thing about bird migration is the question of how they navigate.

Birds seem to have an internal Global Positioning System that allows them to repeat the same migration pattern each year. Scientists are not certain exactly how this is achieved, but it is thought that individual organs have a role in this remarkable ability. A bird's eyes interact with its brain in a region called 'cluster N', which is thought to help the bird determine which way is north. Tiny amounts of iron in the neurons of a bird's inner ear also help in this determination. Some researchers think a bird can smell its way across a flyway. This 'olfactory map' would orientate a bird to terrain and topography. The trigeminal nerve, which connects a bird's beak to its brain, may also help a bird assess its exact location. Researchers think the trigeminal nerve may help birds evaluate the strength of the Earth's magnetic field, which is stronger at the poles and weaker at the equator.

So a bird's physiology is not fully understood in regard to this ability, but we know that it happens. The falcon's eye is drawn to the tiniest movement, hundreds of metres away. A dog's world is coloured and made three-dimensional by its highly developed olfactory ability, said to be two hundred times more acute than ours. A bat, without sight, can fly at speed through a wooded landscape using a kind of radar. Many creatures have ways to survive that we can't use or even understand. However bird migration comes to be understood in time, it will be no less miraculous.

There is surely a likelihood that people possess at least some vestige of some of these senses, or perhaps that our brains may have the potential to acquire some degree of these skills. A person's sense of direction can be both poorly or well developed. Most of us have known people who become lost easily, as well as individuals who somehow instinctively know which direction they should travel. Academics at the University of California have even created a scale as a means of measuring this ability. The Santa Barbara Sense of Direction (SBSOD) was devised in 2002.

I lived for a few years in a derelict fourteenth-century timber house set in a small valley surrounded by Kentish downland. When the sun is setting on the steep banks of the meadow behind the house and the evening shadows lengthen, a series of ancient tracks and paths are revealed. The grass here is very diverse. Every inch of the meadow is a thick mass of tiny species of moss, fungus, and lichen among the grasses. The ground has probably never been ploughed. The soil is chalk with flint and poor clay. When walking across this agreeable space in the stillness of dusk on a summer evening, I become mindful of these animalistic senses. A 'sense of history' begins to take on a more literal meaning. I become acutely aware of my peripheral senses. The transient connection with the past that fleetingly runs through me as I walk here is like the lightest touch of a loved one or a barely perceptible electrical charge. Can I just hear the very last vestiges of reverberating echoes in cascading pressure waves in the ether? Is there order in what I might or might not hear? I try to stay receptive to whatever comes to me in these moments. It becomes a super-reality. This is a mind-expanding place to explore.

A great sommelier will think of every nuance when tasting. Great art of all types is to be found by exploring this place. A fencing champion will focus hard on the peripheries of his vision when in combat, but will always keep his objective to the fore. It is important not to lose sight of the reason for your actions. If a chef creates a meal with a perfect symphony of taste and aroma, the composition on the plate is an innovative balance of form and colour, the textures dance and sing with the flavours in every mouthful. He will still have failed if the customer feels the need for a proper meal when he is back at home. Untapped resources lie at the edges where you're not sure if you can reach.

There is nothing paranormal about this idea. I recall a dinner party in that old house, to which my wife and I had invited, among others, an octogenarian vicar's daughter – who was our church verger – and the local morris dancing warlock, along with his wife. Fabulous people. In the candlelit evening, around the huge open log fire in the distorted wooden house, the conversation eventually turned to things spiritual, mystical, and ghostly. I managed to ruin the evening by commenting that I thought there was something wrong with anybody who believed in ghosts. It was a conversation killer. It was as if I'd said they had ugly children. The evening was over.

Most of us want to believe in the mystical, and looking for inspiration in other worldliness is rewarding, but without remaining rational and accepting your own ignorance, fantasy takes easy flight.

Spending time on a river as we were doing, in the fresh air, away for some time from routine and most of the things of our material world is like changing your winter brogues for easy fitting sandals. You are less restricted. You feel a kind of freedom that allows abstract thoughts to permeate your rested mind.

Mark had busied himself folding and repacking his equipment, maps, and clothes. He is the tidiest of the three of us. He packs everything with great care. His own mountaineering experience has forced on him an efficiency most of us never think about. Dave was sitting comfortably on a log, trying to fix his damaged neoprene footwear with a tiny tube of Epoxy, while I was still on my back on the heat-scorched brown grass long after the cranes had disappeared over the horizon. My eyes might have shut. The late afternoon became evening. Mark created a welcome small rice-based meal around our usual end-of-day fire. It had been the hottest day so far. We were tired and content. We knew that the following day we had a good chance of reaching the sea. That would be a great moment for us. There were mugs of warm wine and talk of the day's events. Later in the evening, three great philosophers emerged and the talk became animated. Eventually, we were talked out. The philosophers became 'sisolophers'. It was time to shut down. Sleep was fitful on the hard ground. The insects reigned.

Days of the week were meaningless, but it was now Wednesday. Our next night would be on a deserted Adriatic beach.

It was another hot day. As we began the day's paddling, Mark rigged up his parasol. The wind began to increase, and it looked like the parasol wasn't up to the task. It soon collapsed. Neither Dave nor I had an umbrella. We smirked at each other watching Mark trying to rescue the elements of his contraption as the wind continued to make his task ever-more frustrating.

The river was now a broad, mainly straight channel. We had no idea what to expect when we would eventually reach the river mouth.

The banks fluctuated between willow and reed. In the reedy sections small huts sprang up along both sides of the river. Each, with reed thatch, had a tall timber mast that could be lowered with pulleys behind into the river. Each mast carried a net, strung into a large square timber frame that would be dipped into the flow to catch fish. The structures are like mini derrick cranes, whose profusion I have described in London. Would the Thames have once had simple fishing contraptions made of natural timber in the round, like these?

At some points a rope, with net attached, was strung across the full width of the river.

There were fishermen ahead now, gesticulating to us. A net was in the water. We could not pass. We would annoy them if we became entangled in their equipment. This could be another angler confrontation with kayakers. We patiently trod water as one of the men pulled himself away from the bank on a simple raft and lifted the net up for us to pass underneath.

The atmosphere was changing. The air felt fresh. The wind was increasing. We were now cruising along quietly with the current gaining strength. There was blazing sun with the occasional scudding cloud in a perfect blue sky. The scintillating horizontal white surf lines were just apparent in the distance.

We had reached the sea.

There was a sentinel lighthouse to the north with tussock dunes behind. The shiny flat sands expanded before us, and the waves broke and raced in shallow sheets towards the scrubby bush forest. Skeletons of bleached driftwood were scattered everywhere.

A flock of flamingos, necks stretched out, in an uneven horizontal formation that echoed the surf, flew across our path. The slow, rhythmical beat of their wings, our paddles, and our hearts left a hypnotic satisfaction to our journey's end.

CHAPTER 5 THE VJOSA

We grounded our kayaks on the sandy curve just south of the river mouth, where racing surf rolled us onto the gleaming flat beach. We jumped out of our kayaks, hurriedly pulled them beyond the waterline, stripped off and we all raced into the sea to congratulate ourselves in a flailing, splashing ensemble, like three bears chasing a fish.

This felt like triumph. After the thrashing around, we flopped over in the cool embrace of the water and let the waves lift us effortlessly up and down. The weightlessness was physical, mental, and spiritual. The sensation of the moment had a stillness. The memory of the euphoria of that afternoon has stayed with me.

We gathered our thoughts about what was next. We had planned to camp nearby. Although this was the psychological end of the journey, we still had two more days to explore another 20 miles of coastline down to Vlorë.

The wind was steady, and waves were crashing in at a height well over a metre in continuous rows of frothy white-capped barrels. We were unsure if we could get out beyond these rollers with fully laden kayaks and avoid capsizing.

We decided that capsizing wouldn't much matter here, so when we had regained our composure, we planned to head south for a mile or so. Heading straight out would be difficult, but travelling parallel to the breakers would be a serious challenge.

Mark pushed out far enough to avoid the worst of the breaking waves, but both Dave and I, after a few hundred metres, went in without much chance of rolling upright. We had spent hours practising our kayak rolls in a swimming pool back at home, but that bore no comparison to here with all our equipment in and on our kayaks – and these conditions. Dave and I clung onto our upturned kayaks and managed to turn them back in the brief periods between the breaking waves. We let the warm water of the rhythmic waves push us into the shallow waters without attempting to climb back into our boats. Pushing along in the shallows for a while parallel to the beach was a pleasant experience. I feared that one of my deck covers over the rear compartment had let in water. Unfortunately, it was my bedding.

We were well away from the river by now, and ready to camp, so we signalled to each other and dragged our boats out of the warm sea and up on top of the sandy ridge before the scrubby thickets of bush that ran to the south as far as we could see.

The plastic debris along the riverbank was not as evident along the coast. This was idyllic. Looking south, the perspective of the gradual curve of the ochre beach windswept with foamy spray had a vanishing point that was hidden in the haze.

I've read that sea air and sea spray are full of negative ions that improve our ability to absorb oxygen by neutralising damaging free radicals, the positive ions. It is at least easy to feel the energising effect of this environment.

Dave and I sat on the sand looking out over the rumbling scene of the sea while Mark made a scout for camp. After a short while, Mark's grinning head appeared through the dark green overgrowth behind us. He beckoned us in.

✻

The brush was short and like tinder. Largely evergreen bushes with twisting gnarled trunks. Mark had found a cosy spot in a bowl-shaped sandy clearing, just right to bed down in later.

We were almost out of water and our filter could do nothing with sea water. The map showed some roads a mile south, so it was decided that Dave and I would set off with water carriers, leaving Mark to tidy up and look after the kit. He couldn't light a campfire because the low wood thicket was so obviously a fire hazard.

We walked on the harder wet section of the beach for easier traction. The heat was becoming manageable. A refreshing breeze lightened our heels. After half an hour, the landscape inland gradually became brackish marsh with less scrub. We saw a row of streetlights some way inland, and a few animal tracks led through the grassy marshland. We made our way towards this sign of people and were soon on a sandy path with wheel tracks. There were now tall pine trees in the distance. The track became a concrete road, crazed with tough plants growing through the cracks. Some timber huts appeared, and we were soon up to the lamps. There were strange 1960s-looking architectural ruins of dusty concrete and painted blocks with dilapidated signage, letters missing or hanging askew. There was a network of roads and pavements, all cracked and blistered with creeping moss and vines competing to hide them. Plywood panelling on the huts had friable, peeling paint blowing in the wind, and the green paint on the lamps had come off in a leopard-skin patchwork. This was how I imagine Chernobyl feels. Deserted, once busy, nature ever reclaiming.

Dave questioned why we River Rats so often stumble across surreal film sets. I spotted some movement near one of the buildings and we headed that way. A tall, very dark man, possibly in his seventies, appeared. He wore a wide-brimmed hat over thick white hair. He wore shorts with a dirty white vest and rubber boots. He was surprised to see us but seemed quite pleased.

We did our best to exchange greetings and he could see from our empty cargo what we were after. He had a little English, so as we walked behind him in the direction of, presumably, a tap, he explained with much aid of sign language a little about this strange locale.

He was the caretaker of this place. He told us that he had always worked here. A disused communist party holiday village. It must have been a long time since it was used.

The politics of Albania has a ghastly and violent recent past. Our friend here would have been looking after officials from the brutal regime of Enver Hoxha, whose 40-year reign was a time when many thousands of Albanian-perceived dissidents were executed and tens of thousands were forced into concentration camps. Freedoms of all kinds – religious, travel and speech – were savagely curtailed. The Yugoslav wars caused further difficulties with an exodus into the country from those fleeing Serb forces in Kosovo. Only in this century, with ambition to join the EU and accepted NATO membership from 2009, has any improvement in living standards been achieved.

When we viewed the position of our septuagenarian caretaker within the context of this history, and the turmoil that he had endured, it glaringly highlighted the privilege and stability that we three have only ever taken for granted.

The political history of this broken-down resort gave it a sinister presence. There may have been people once playing basketball on the court in front of us that were on holiday here as a reward for their cruelty. As these thoughts came to me, the air began to feel bad.

The old man helped us fill several water containers and continued to try and communicate with us about how this dilapidated collection of buildings once thronged with people and activity. He was chain-smoking the whole time we were together, but always generously offered us a smoke before he lit up. He would have been a young man when this tired place was in its heyday. He could only have seen degeneration since those times. His bodily vigour would have declined in tandem. Perhaps he would see out his days here and the decay would start to reverse after the passing of his generation, when, let's hope, stability and freedom are secure.

He sent us on our way with a languorous wave of a lean arm and a broad smile on his crag-riven stubbly face.

It was a long walk back to base and the weight of the water made it a trial. We were back before dark and were able to enjoy an evening chat and feed before laying out our sleeping mats for the night. I'd have to put up with a damp sleeping bag, which I continually repositioned through the night in an effort to keep to the dry parts.

There was little moonlight that night. We could see a thousand tiny eyes shining through the thickets around us. We tried to identify some of these creatures, but nothing was ever visible when we directed a torch towards them. We could, however, detect movement and shapes in the near dark. We could hear distant dogs barking. Insects buzzed and the soft, soporific chorus of the crickets soothed us as the sea crooned its nighttime incantation. The wind was calming. We slept soundly on the soft sand.

On waking, we found all manner of animal tracks in the sand, especially around our cooking equipment. A series of distinctive tortoise tracks circled Mark's sleeping spot. While we had slept, nocturnal life had been busy.

CHAPTER 5 THE VJOSA

The ecology of the Vlorë Bay is of some significance. There are several academic papers that point out the diversity of the forest, scrubland, dunes, sandbanks, and the rocky mountainous environment of the area. I could recognise sedum, a selection of wild brassicas, and Echinophora. To his delight, Mark found a wonderful white flower, a sea daffodil, with petals like the crystals of a snowflake. There were tiny molluscs and a profusion of butterflies and crickets, all of which would make worthy scientific study.

Yesterday's sea was a charging frothing beast, bounding inland with arching leaps, roaring and clawing at the air. This morning that beast was purring in reclining slumber as we slid out quietly over its velvety pelt, our bows effortlessly parting the water's surface, like fingers running through a mink stole.

The sensation that comes with the first float of the day was amplified this morning and gently uplifting. Mark rigged up his parasol. It was going to be hot. We had seen that a large lagoon bulged inland from the sea some 15 kilometres down the coast. There is an island in the lagoon, on which lies a thirteenth-century monastery, where we were hoping to stay that night.

The going was easy. The light maintained a pale haze throughout the day. The occasional island appeared a few miles off the coast. It was easy to anthropomorphise their shapes as sleeping giants floating in the sunshine.

The colour of the water fluctuated with the underlying current in the sea and the landscape behind and above. If I were painting the sea here, my palette would start with cobalt blue and phthalo green. I would require cerulean blue for the greener tints and a tiny quantity of ultramarine where darker, dramatic streaks floated in strata formation across the horizon. The yellower vistas occur with reflection from the putty-yellow cliffs. I would need raw sienna for this. All the while, the tones would be adjusted with titanium white in varying degrees. The delicious thirst-quenching translucency of it all would mean that the paint on my canvas would be built up in many thin layers of tinted glaze. Ground colour must permeate the washes to give depth and vibrancy. An opaquer waterscape was sometimes visible. These areas, and the whiter highlights, would be a thicker impasto application, which would also lend texture to the effect.

The surreal colours revealing light and the quietness of the morning was like gliding along inside a Matisse painting. Our mood often mirrors the landscape we travel through. We were quiet, reflective, passively observant.

We paddled past low cliffs and rocky bays with long sandy crescent beaches. We hadn't yet seen anyone. We pushed in to one of these bays for a break from the heat. Many curious multicoloured goats unexpectedly made their way to inspect us invaders. Mark did his best to approach the beasts, but they avoided close contact. He pursued one of the younger ones across the beach, his hat flying off as he ran. I'm not sure what he would have done if he'd caught up with his quarry.

We made a makeshift sun shelter and huddled together to study Google Earth images to see when and how to access the lagoon. As usual, we tended to defer to Mark in all things navigational. Despite the temperature, Mark scrabbled around in his hold and brought out the tiny stove, kettle, and some biscuits for a reviving brew. Tea seems to refresh in nearly all circumstances. In Cherry-Garrard's The Worst Journey in the World, when almost all was lost as Scott's doomed team battled to survive starvation and exhaustion in the Antarctic, there was no question that they would continue to drink tea.

There was little distance to cover before camp, so we enjoyed the unhurried ease of the day. We made a plan, climbed into our cockpits, then, using our paddles like punts, pushed out over the shallow beach towards the site that we guessed could offer access to the lagoon. We arrived at about midday and landed where a series of sluice gates were used to regulate the water levels in the lagoon some 30 metres across the isthmus.

※

Mark had identified some old military installation at the top of the adjacent cliff. We all scrambled up to investigate. It was a defensive gun placement, with a dome-shaped bunker in front. A dank tunnel at the back had a series of technical instructions painted neatly with a sign writer's brush on a flat section of render. The lichen-clad concrete surface was streaked with rust. Mark was confident the gun placement was a World War II relic. The goats now found shelter here. The bunker, however, was familiar. We had seen many of these along our journey. Hoxha fanatically built almost 200,000 of these in what was called 'bunkerisation'. That equates to six bunkers for every square kilometre in the country. Albania was still technically at war with Greece until 1987. Invasion was thought likely.

We carried our kayaks over this short stretch. The land-locked body of water appeared with glinting brightness in front of us. This was Narta Lagoon, and the island is called Zvërnec Island. The water's surface was black and shiny, like polished marble. The wooded island was only a few hundred metres offshore from where we set down to refloat. If I'd still had my paints out, Brunswick green would have done nicely for the pine trees. We could see from the grassy shore, where hard sand gradually gave way to something of a powder-sized grain, that the lagoon was sitting in muddy silt. There was a strong smell of methane. Plastic debris was visible here and there.

The water was only a few inches deep at the shore, so we decided to wade in, pulling our boats behind us until we could float. The mud became softer and softer. The sandy silt at the edge was like walking in peanut butter. It soon became like walking in Marmite. Each pace was sucking our feet and legs in the vacuum created as we pulled to retract each step. The stinking black mud was reaching our knees. After 50 or 60 metres of this, the going became tedious. Dave wanted to go back and porter along the shore. Mark was keen to keep going on methodically. We made continued efforts to float. This became very frustrating when, having struggled to get into our cockpits, it was, after all, still not possible to float. The slime was covering everything. Clambering in and out, slipping around in the stench was tiresome. A few fucks and bollocks were slung about. I tried to outline our options logically. We were by now Englishmen out in the savage midday sun like mad dogs. Mark was confident that a deeper channel was nearby. I didn't much care which option we went for, but possibly swung slightly to an onward vote. Of all of us, Mark is the more insistent character, and we decided to follow his view. I offered to go on for ten minutes to test the going, leaving the others to rest. We just kept going. We were not yet halfway and could still turn back. This was no place for any boat. We had no way of knowing. Good fortune arrived and at last a change of water colour revealed some water about a foot deep that we could paddle through. Even then, it was ten minutes of a part-paddle part-heave punt that saw us on into clear water over a metre deep.

The island was near, and thankfully there were no mud banks to deal with as we pulled up on large smooth boulders, surrounded by stiff green reeds, on the pine-wooded island. From where we landed there was no sign of any habitation, but we knew that the island was only 300 by 400 metres, so we must be near the monastery.

※

We secured the kayaks and did our best to clean the worst of the mud from ourselves and the boats. We were now doused from head to foot in a thin slimy film of eau de crap. The island is a small hill, so we set off through the wood, glad of the shade, to find the monastery. Crepuscular rays shimmered and danced along with us in an enchanting, ever-changing kaleidoscopic display along the woodland floor.

There were black squirrels in the tall cypress and a collection of, apparently, tame rabbits hopping on mossy banks among the pine litter. The seaside birdsong was replaced by a persistent twittering of finches and tits. I could identify the 'watch-winding' punctuation between the wheezy notes of a siskin.

We quickly reached the high point of the island and then descended along well-trodden paths to the other side. We approached the monastery from its rear. From this side it looked like a single rectangular farm building. Once we made our way to the front, we could see a much more sophisticated and very aged Byzantine church construction. There were several other, largely two-storey, buildings creating a large kind of grassy courtyard. This is known as St Mary's Monastery, or the Monastery of Dormition of Theotokos Mary. The church's low-level construction with its seven Byzantine arch colonnade façades stood in powerful squat defiance to Hoxha's purges, which it had thankfully survived.

We could see a laden washing line next to one of the dormitory buildings, so Dave walked over to see if we could find anyone. He found a hefty middle-aged man with thick iron-grey hair and a kindly manner. Dave was beckoned up an external stone staircase to the man's apartments, where Dave was offered the key to access the church. The man had a little English and Dave thought that he had explained about the kayaks and that we would prefer to clean up before entering the house of God. It seemed that he was OK with us bedding down on the island and he offered us bottles of water.

We walked the short coastal route back to the boats and paddled round to the monastery where we planned to pull up near the buildings. The island is connected by an old wooden footbridge. A new one, built with an extremely beautiful snaking design – the floor slats still with the fresh-sawn appearance of new timber – was 300 metres long, and was well advanced in construction.

We left our kayaks near the footbridge and went back to explore our options. Dave's newfound friend, not a priest, gestured to us that we must hide our boats. He took us behind one of the buildings to a disused concrete basketball court. He was happy for us to stay but didn't want to advertise this to others. This was, after all, a well-known tourist destination locally. Our offer of some payment was refused. We all shook hands heartily. We laid out our kit on the mossy crazed concrete of the court and found a tap to effect a proper clean-up of bodies, shoes, clothes, and spirits. The sun was now losing its midday strength but was plenty enough to dry everything off quickly.

It was early afternoon, hunger was biting, so we decided to leave ecclesiastical exploration until later, and walk to the mainland in search of a café. We found the cleanest clothes available, then sauntered along the footbridge to the mainland. Plenty of fishermen were busy on the footbridge.

There was a caravan parked at the base of the bridge with tables and umbrellas. We had a refreshing drink and left with directions to a restaurant. The walk was twenty minutes, and we were soon at a table with a thick starched white tablecloth under a leafy pergola.

Dave tried his best teeth-glinting charm on our lovely young waitress, who brought us rows of pan-fried bream, fresh from the lagoon, with a wonderful assortment of delicious oily salads, all washed down with very cold beer. The chat was relaxed. We were starting to exhale, as the physical challenge of our trip was now over.

We ended up in a conversation, in English, with one of the owners of the establishment about the litter, especially plastic waste that was visible almost everywhere. He made an interesting point that not so long ago, under communism, there was almost no plastic. People brought their own baskets to the shop. They even brought their own ceramic vessels for wet goods, like honey or wine. Western goods were not available. The necessities of poverty meant that things were repaired repeatedly. When a machine had run its day, the composite parts had value and were stripped down and reused. An admirable ethos brought on by need.

The profusion of insects and smaller mammals everywhere is also an ironic benefit of poverty. Much of the farming and horticulture is small scale and farmers cannot afford the expensive insecticides and chemicals that are in use all over Europe, and their country has a richer, more biodiverse countryside. Wealth squanders riches that poverty preserves.

Before the invasion of Ukraine, we had tentative plans to kayak the length of Lake Baikal in Russia. Mark had found a book, *Kayak Adventure in Siberia*, by Detlev Henschel, and others, describing their recent adventure on the lake. The same issue is discussed in their book. There is no rubbish collection in that part of Russia and it seems that the more beautiful and visited spots on Baikal are littered with muck and rubbish. They point out that aside from the fact that hardly any rubbish was produced under communism, everything could be reused. After the collapse of the Soviet Union, the rubbish suddenly appeared; paper and bottles are no longer recycled, and there are now plastic bottles and fast-food packaging to contend with too. They talk about the 'new Russians', who dump everything in the countryside, unaware that they are littering, as they have already got their work cut out trying to stay alive.

We settled the bill. As before, the meal was cheaper than a sandwich at St Pancras, and we walked slowly back along the dusty road.

When we arrived back at the bridge, there was a group of young men loitering around, smoking and jeering. In the middle of the group, perched on the timber bridge handrail, was a young priest in black Greek Orthodox attire. The air carried the distinctive herbal earthy scent of cannabis, which I always think carries a hint of diesel. To our great surprise, a joint was passed on to our priest, who took a deep toke before passing it to the next louche disciple on the handrail. There seemed to be no embarrassment at all as we walked past them. They were all male, and although there was nothing threatening about them, there was a kind of disdain and discourtesy about their curt acknowledgements.

We stopped with some of the fishermen, who were also not keen to communicate. We seemed to be under suspicion. Further along, on an elegantly curved section of the bridge, we interrupted a photographer and a bride in full white wedding garb. The bride was sometimes standing, sometimes kneeling and then, feet hanging off the bridge, she let the train of the extravagant dress trail in the lagoon. As we walked past while she sat, she looked at us over her shoulder. She was a dark beauty with a confident alluring smile. Our bridge was obviously an acknowledged beauty spot. We glanced back at our weed-smoking cleric, and could see his distinctive headgear, known as a kalimavkion, nodding away with his flock of miscreants.

We could see an assortment of wading birds in the distance: sandpipers, curlews, and the awkwardly designed spoonbill. In the far distance, flamingos, their heads underwater, were filtering the food offered by the life-rich salt marsh mud of the lagoon.

Once back at our basketball camp, we decided to have a look around the monastery church. The church was unlocked, so we could enter and explore freely. The larger buildings surrounding the church, presumably the dormitory and working quarters for the monks, do not possess the very ancient feel of the church. The church is a low, strong building, which lacks the sophistication of Christian Orthodox buildings I have seen in Istanbul and Balkan capitals. The heavy stones of the walls and floor are knitted together tightly, like the kernels of a corn cob, but the outer surface has only been crudely worked. The colonnade, with its seven arches, each a slightly different size, has a kind of unprofessional look to its construction and reminds me of eleventh-century Norman architecture at home in small Kentish villages. The weather and time have ravaged the stone columns so that some now have an hourglass look. The capitals are so worn away, I couldn't tell if they were composite or Corinthian. The bases have very poor concrete repairs, and a reinforcement bar runs across every arch. The overall design has the unmistakable Eastern Orthodox style of cruciform plan with central drum tower. There is a simple gable bell tower on the extended gable of the west end of the building.

Inside, the feeling of reverence is all pervading. There is no stained glass, but a warm light rakes across every surface. Glowing gilded icons reflect colour and stare at us with calm repose. An icon of Mary is most prominent. There is a tall, highly decorated screen, called a templon, separating the altar from the body of the church. The timber is carved on every surface. The gilt and colour depiction of the apostles and saints, all muted by craquelure and aged patina, is laid out around the screen in an approximation of symmetry. In front and above, around the inner face of the drum, were plain windows, reducing the cool dimness. Everything is at a small scale; the top of the tower is not especially high and the stone work becomes coarser and more uneven.

We all felt the need to whisper, and hats were off. The exquisite charm of the place was spellbinding.

※

That evening, we strolled again along the footbridge to the most dazzling sunset. There were a few people who were enjoying the same activity. Walking across the water - like kayaking - prompts a synergy between atmosphere and mood. All was calm and warmth. At home, the Victorian concept of the pier stretching into the sea, and perambulation to take in the air has largely disappeared. A walk with water on all sides is a mind-clearing experience.

We had so far been spared any serious trouble with the demon mosquito, but Mark was pointing out that with the brackish water and larvae-rich mud flats, tonight might be the end of that luck. Mark had energy enough remaining to scout about for various suitable objects to squat on for the last of the evening. We thought that a fire was not appropriate here, so we sat around a small battery lamp to focus on as the apricot glow in the sky very slowly dimmed. To everyone's relief, the plague of mosquitos never materialised.

It grew into an evening when time distorted. Time can speed up or slow down, depending on circumstance. Memory too can be recalled in a slow-motion version, as when recollecting a dangerous event. This was an evening of distorted time. The ardent tangerine glow in the sky bathed us with generosity. A kind of freewheeling hope that spun a long yarn, looping and stretching like teasing out pliant dough, softly oscillated, massaging the optimism. In the halcyon kaftan days, this would have been called 'digging a good vibe'.

We slipped into our sleeping bags and carried on chatting as a slight cool drifted over the melancholy lagoon. Our murmuring conversation was occasionally invigorated by a catch of excitement. An element of over refreshment with the wine spurred on some very memorable and fantastic conversation. We chanced on the subject of pole vaulting. Dave was a Sports Science student at Loughborough, where top vaulters were training. Mark recalled Bob Seagren and Wolfgang Nordwig of the 1970s, when the sport began to gain glamour. I had even tried some rudimentary pole vaulting.

This subject grew into a hot debate on the correct methodology of good vaulting: the exact timing of weight transfer and balance. Dave crawled out of his sleeping bag to find a length of driftwood and was demonstrating all this in his underpants in the dark. They say that a little knowledge is a dangerous thing. If an actual vaulting pole had been lying around, there is no knowing what Dave might have attempted.

 Later that evening after sleep's veil had barely settled, our opposition, the priests, were streaming onto the basketball court, limbering up energetically, their ridiculous-looking hats askew. Dave was running on the spot, Mark leapt up and down like a pogo. I was squat-thrusting on the sidelines. The bonfire scent of many spliffs was choking the air. The game began. Knees whirred like whirligigs. After years under black cassocks, skirts lifted, the pale legs of the clergy, elongated and etiolated by phototropic endeavour, yelled, 'Hallelujah, I've seen the light!'

A cohort of sullen posing young supporters looked on nonchalantly. We were being outrun. The ground underfoot became squelching mud. They could fly, but we could hardly make ground. A beautiful dusky young woman with Slavic eyes suddenly tore along the centre line in a full billowing white wedding dress; Mark was miraculously right with her. His diminutive size and agility with her speed wove dodging through the defenders, like a pair of rugby forwards, dramatically breaking through a three-quarter line.

Miraculously, the white goddess then slam-dunked a winning glorious goal into the hoop. The moody entourage were finally animated and cheering resentfully. Dave vaulted high over the chain-link fence, his pole wobbling and crashing as he punched the air in delight while descending onto a bed of a thousand writhing live bream. The bride walked back along the footbridge. Two flame-pink flamingos had settled on her raven hair, necks and heavy bills creating a symmetrical heart. Mark emerged triumphantly from the monastery colonnade, proudly bearing a bunch of snow-headed daffodils. He was followed by a procession of tortoises, their necks outstretched, each one carrying a single lit candle on its ancient rocky back, waxy drippings decoratively spilling onto their crusty shells. The crashing waves cheered. Tall rushes swayed. A donkey brayed. A blood hound bayed.

Our last day was a gentle time of winding down and relaxation. We had seen on the map a few beachfront hotels just a few miles south on the edge of Vlorë. We paddled onto the first hotel beach we saw and booked in. We were the only guests. We made arrangements with our man in Tirana to collect the kayaks in the morning and we booked a taxi to take us back to Saranda for the ferry to Corfu.

Journey's End

Journeys can conclude under diverse circumstances and conditions. This paddle finished with a blissful satisfaction. Dave has this to say about it:

Our arrival at Vlorë made me ponder our journey's end. Are Hollywood endings exclusively celluloid, or can adventures really finish so magnificently?

The magnitude of achievement can often be too great to be absorbed in the short moments of completion. Instead, the rather lame, 'It hasn't sunk in yet' or 'I'm over the moon' comes out.

I had such feelings after crossing Panama from the Caribbean to the Pacific through uncharted jungle, and the Alps via the 'Haute Route' in winter.

They were adrenaline-fuelled times, shared with the finest companions anyone could hope for. I do not mean to diminish those adventures, or their completion, but it takes a lifetime of reflection, often in quiet moments years after the event, to fully absorb and reflect on such intensity.

The Vjosa was somehow different.

The glass-like Aegean Sea merged with the cloudless midday sky. Each paddle 'plosh' echoed in the still air as we rounded the final headland. No 'false summit' of further distant bays to navigate. Our hotel was the nearest and it beckoned like a jewel embedded in the horseshoe bay.

Final easy strokes glided us through crystal shallows that lapped the manicured beach, a secure resting place for kayaks and kit. We retired to the dappled light on the restaurant terrace. A full complement of welcoming staff served crisp cold beers and an array of freshly cooked seafood. No other guests in sight. Glasses chinked in celebration.

On this occasion the reward came all at once – in that instant.

That afternoon, leading into the night, we walked around Vlorë. It is a modern town with the evidence of its ancient roots largely overrun by recent growth. Giant Soviet bronze sculptures adorn the town's municipal areas.

Soviet sculpture is strangely joyful. The style is called social realism, idealising with realistic imagery, the rising proletariat's noble struggle against capitalism. The elevated status of workers and political thinkers is usually depicted in motion, striding with pride into the (then) new liberating era of communism. Vlorë has one especially huge bronze statue depicting such a scene. There is something of a *Marvel* superhero about the look of all this. Mark and Dave were shamelessly hopping around the installation, posing to mimic the chest-puffing poses soaring at 10 metres above them.

The debate about Britain's colonial statuary present in every major city is gaining momentum. What does the future hold for all the bronze and stone Soviet era statues in Albania?

We enjoyed the evening trying to chat with locals at open-air bars in the Adriatic heat of the soulless town centre, the busy port of Vlorë nearby.

We returned home after a pleasant night in Corfu. The naturalist Gerald Durrell, who wrote so much on the natural history on Corfu, would have recognised with equal delight much of the fauna and flora of the Albania we had explored. Long may it be preserved.

CHAPTER 6

LONDON TOWN
AUGUST 2018

A city is more than its buildings

The world's major conurbations have often emerged on the banks of a mighty river. The Thames is a minnow in size but is a leaping salmon in historical significance.

The Thames is the reason that London is in this place. It was swimming upstream in these fertile waters that the seed of this city found fertile ground to germinate. London and the Thames is much written about. *Thames: Sacred River* by Peter Ackroyd, one of many others, is an absorbing read.

Mark had organised a day jaunt by kayak – unusually for us, with two guides – that took us in sturdy double kayaks from Battersea Church to the Cutty Sark at Greenwich. Although, this was not a 'Rat Journey', and was just a day trip, we were together and the day was a great success.

It was just Mark's party that made up that day's complement, comprising himself, his sons, Robert and Graham, Dave, my wife, Kay, and three of Mark's work colleagues. We assembled at nine o'clock in the morning at St Mary's Church in Battersea on a cold, drizzly Thursday morning, just as the tide began to turn seaward.

The guides were cheerful Irishmen in their twenties. They were quite expert, and one of these capable fellows had not long returned from a solo kayak trip circumnavigating the island of Ireland. We took a basic safety briefing, which may as well have been in Urdu. Even if I could have heard him above the rain, I wouldn't have been able to understand his quick words and broad Irish accent. He must have had a former life as a race commentator.

Each couple in turn, kitted up with spray deck and buoyancy aid, slid into the two cockpits, then floated out to tread water, ready for the off. It was a little choppy as we departed, and the guides immediately started telling the company a little about significant landmarks, which are at every sight in all directions. With the wind rising, rain and spray increasing, we couldn't hear a thing. We all pretended to understand them.

We have all seen terrestrial London, even riverine London, but slinking along in low-level kayaks through such a well-known urban water thoroughfare offers a different perspective on the old town. We were speedily through Battersea Bridge, then the wedding cake pastel-decorated Albert Bridge, and past the

Buddhist Peace Pagoda looking over the river in Battersea Park. Mark pointed out the cormorants, one on every buoy that we encountered. This was the case right through to Greenwich. They have greatly increased in number over the last twenty years. Despite the general river degradation throughout the country and E. coli being found in ever greater concentrations recently, Thames Water claims that the Thames is the cleanest river running through any major city. Many fish have returned, which has brought in the cormorants. Famously, salmon are even recorded occasionally. There was no drying off with umbrella wings today for the cormorants on the buoys. They are efficient fishers, hated by anglers, who call them the Black Death. They are upright and look proud, with reptilian green eyes and waterproof feathers with the beetle's oily gleam of shimmering black-green. In no time at all, we were under Chelsea Bridge and paddling past Battersea Power Station.

To me, the power station means *Dr Who*, crime dramas and low-budget TV. It will never be a film set now, any more than Pink Floyd will again wire a giant flying pig to the iconic chimneys.

The work of Sir Giles Gilbert Scott colours the architectural identity of the capital. His iconic K6 telephone kiosk has echoes in the repetitive rectangular shapes and motifs of the power station. These disappearing telephone boxes are often bemoaned when compared to the replacements, which are also now obsolete or gone. There is a monumental feeling to the huge edifice he created that was built through the 1930s. The steel structure has a thin skin of specially made 'golden brown pressed brick'. Rarely is so much brick seen in one place.

The international thirst for London investment apartments in the end held sway, so more imaginative schemes, pondered over many years for the property, were dropped. The power station-selling agents claim that it has created 'the most exciting and innovative mixed-use neighbourhoods in the world'. I don't think so.

The blocky glass buildings crammed up against the old power station look like giant container ships that have docked alongside. The appeal of the geometric monolith is now totally lost. The regeneration of the whole area is creating a new landscape of urban canyons and gorges. Gleaming glass abounds. The skyline had the inevitable host of cranes with their towering derricks jutting up at all angles, like a bad haircut on a windy day. The Americans have even relocated their embassy in the shadow of the power station.

The current was comfortable, but passing larger vessels, both leisure boats and more traditional working vessels, left us bobbing in their wakes. We were careful to aim bow forward for the larger of these onslaughts. A capsize would be uncomfortable at best and could be a danger with these other vessels nearby.

Parliament appeared on the north side, with Lambeth Palace on the south. Since 1066, thirty-eight monarchs have been crowned at Westminster Abbey. That seems like very few for a thousand-year span. The richly carved surface decoration of Westminster Palace was darkened by the rain. It rises right to the riverbank. From our kayaks it seemed taller and longer than the pedestrian view. Sir Charles Barry's yellow limestone Gothic fancy is, and has been for a long time, one of the most familiar images of any kind around the world. It is an enduring image, but any grandeur is lessened by its endless association with mugs, key rings, and tourist trinkets. Like everyone else, we rated ourselves as much better than mere tourists.

One of our guides pointed out that the clock tower is not called Big Ben but should be referred to as St Stephen's Tower; he told us that only the bell should be called Big Ben. As I drew up alongside Mark and Graham, I was pedantically able to explain that the nickname 'Big Ben' should correctly only refer to the larger of the five bells in the tower and it is known as the Great Bell of Westminster. Music excepted, there are very few sounds that resound through history and have meaning across the globe, but the sound of Big Ben has truly achieved that celebrated status. Throughout my life, there has always been a time in the night at some point, by accident rather than design, that I have heard on the World Service the familiar, strangely faltering dong of the bell as the hammer drops onto the cast bronze, once for every hour on the hour, at intervals of exactly four and a half seconds. If you were to believe in empire, now more a cause of shame than pride, then the sound of the bell during the period of Britain's colonial heyday must have seemed, to the British at least, like a patient maternal call to order or a paternal reassurance of protection.

Next door a more recent parliamentary building has been built over the road from the clock tower. Known as Portcullis House, it opened in 1992. The design and material specification is lofty and expensive, but that hasn't stopped them looking unspeakably ugly. Strange dome-headed cylinders with central chimney-pot-looking structures, like industrial kilns, that would sit nicely in Stoke-on-Trent. Maybe they recycle all the hot air that's produced over the road?

We approached Westminster Bridge from the south side. As we drew near, the perspective on entering the furthest aperture, with the repetitive arches of the steel structure and the Victorian lamps visible along the Embankment, I was reminded of the dolphins' curving backs we had seen in the Moray Firth. The magnificent aquatic beasts that decorate these ornate Victorian lamps are, at least in heraldic terminology, said to be dolphins. More axolotl than fish, with half-human heads, they lithely wrap around the shaft of the lamp. Nothing like a dolphin, the wrought iron castings are usually painted black and have a serious, weighty feel, typical of Victorian London. I am comfortable around this ornament. It generates a fake nostalgia. I was never there, but like *Dad's Army*, its memory provides comfort.

Shortly after Westminster Bridge, we were in choppy water, looking up at the steel circus Ferris wheel that is the London Eye on the South Bank. It towers over County Hall, the Edwardian baroque headquarters of the old Greater London Council.

I have long been part of the daily migrating mass of those travelling into the City from the provinces. The cars, trucks, trains, bicycles, and all begin to infiltrate through every orifice, artery, and vein from five o'clock in the morning, like a steadily constricting iris of another giant eye coming into sharp focus as the day begins to lay down its challenges.

On Victoria Embankment on the north side, there is a small memorial to the man, who, you could argue, saved more London lives than anyone in history. Joseph Bazalgette built the embankment, but more vitally for the health of the residents, he designed and built London's first proper sewers. This was the nation's response to the Great Stink during the summer of 1858, when parliament had to be suspended due to the stench. We saw evidence all along the river of the £5-billion Thames Tideway scheme to finally upgrade London's sewers to meet the anticipated demand.

The festival of concrete, which is the Royal Festival Hall, was now on the south side. The 1961 Southbank Centre, a successful attempt to create a great cultural centre, is considered an extreme example of the architectural brutalism of the age. I appreciate the attention to detail. Before we all spent time driving through so many hideously placed municipal car parks of similar construction technique, the concrete surface decoration of cast shuttering ply appeared clean and refreshing. Concrete often does not age well, but the patina of these structures is calming, and the composition of the whole collection is satisfying.

The drizzle continued to cast a thin veil of smudge over all we surveyed. Our hair was wet, our hands cold and red. Even here, as I trailed my wrinkled fingers in the murky water, I was reminded of the life-giving force of water: nature's most abundant treasure. In the end, all life, including great cities, depends on all things natural.

The architecture of the city has a thrusting confidence. It cares little for what people think; it's not afraid of failure. Capitalist organic growth is all around. The offices and the city living quarters are squeezed tightly together and are forced upward. Buildings seem to spring up with no regard for their neighbours. The queue-jumping of each successive development jostling to have a better waterfront view, crowding out each stage, is very un-British. The medieval bridges of Europe, well preserved in Florence and Venice, were crowded with cantilevered shops and timber add-ons of all types. London bridges were like this once. Now this kind of haphazard development occurs at every opportunity on the waterfront. Apart from scale, it's not so different.

We had the twin draws of Tate Modern, the former Bankside Power Station on our right, and Wren's St Paul's Cathedral on our left. The power station, another Gilbert Scott masterpiece, opened in 2000 as a prestigious modern art gallery.

Tate Modern sits altogether more comfortably with its neighbours than its sister in Battersea. The adjoining buildings are carefully linked in colour and detail of form. The startling Millennium Bridge, floating in the air across the river like the vertebrae of a sun-burnished dinosaur skeleton, is perfectly aligned to create a terminating vista of the south facade of St Paul's Cathedral. The gallery, with its tall central chimney and regular translucent glass roof addition, confidently displays classical symmetry.

Man and architecture seem to be predisposed to symmetry. It is there in the human form and everywhere in nature. Classical architecture is based on symmetry. Even when viewing an asymmetric pleasing composition of turrets and castellation of a favourite Capability Brown-landscaped stately home, some consider the reflective symmetry in an adjoining lake to elevate the whole scene for this reason. Even where symmetry is not apparent, the potential is usually there. What can't be split evenly in two?

Asymmetry is altogether more pleasing. It was a cornerstone, in architecture at least, of the Romantic Movement that swept Europe from the middle of the eighteenth century. Romanticism also had expression in music and literature. Classicism is order and safety. Romanticism is freedom and uncertainty. Modernist architecture has often embraced asymmetry, and much of London's skyline seen from the river is a celebration of this: The Shard, The Walkie-Talkie, The Quill, and the National Theatre. On the other hand, along with Tate Modern, we have St Paul's Cathedral, The Gherkin, St George's Wharf and Canary Wharf, to name just a few that proclaim the surety of symmetry. Almost all towns and cities, with organic growth over time, offer only asymmetric vistas when viewed as a whole.

In our ordinary lives symmetry provides order in the chaos that surrounds us all. Everyday rituals create easy satisfaction in their symmetry: laying the table, making the bed, arranging cushions on a sofa, or planting rows of vegetables. Asymmetry offers surprise, chance, and passion. Flowers from your garden, arranging food on a plate, dance, even the tilt of a head are all simple expressions of asymmetry.

Composition might be deliberately unbalanced to create tension, and a composition will vary depending on the message you are trying to communicate, but compositional balance, where your eye is not drawn to one area at the exclusion of others, is also a kind of symmetry.

Any ocean-going vessel – kayaks included – that does not display symmetry would be a strange craft indeed.

St Paul's finally became visible. I can't look at St Paul's without picturing the iconic wartime newspaper image where the defiant dome symbolises Britain's resolve and strength when all around was the fire and destruction of blitzkrieg.

We've all become accustomed to high-rise cities. When built in 1711, the cathedral was the tallest building in London, and remained so until the BT Tower was opened in 1965.

Shakespeare's Globe incongruously appeared to our right. A faithful reconstruction of the Elizabethan Globe Theatre, with its tall white sides and thatched roof, put me in mind of what a seventeenth-century Emirates football stadium may have looked like. The crowds in those days would have spilled out to view the same river as we were riding. The river itself would have been little different.

The Thames offers distinct meanings to people at different times in their lives. Some, at times of inner turmoil, will see a quiet continuum of stolidity, offering some stillness and comfort, like a friend who silently sits close when you need solace. Others will reflect on the jangling rhythm of the choppy glint of the dancing ripples, living joyfully for now, without care for what lies beneath. Some have chosen it to be their grave, which is ritually sacrificial and commendatory. The secrets scattered and buried along the riverbed have their own stories. Some will resurface; others will remain locked in sediment that will one day be rock, beyond the times of man. We slid under Southwark Bridge with London Bridge very nearby.

*

A few years ago, an incident occurred on the river when a knife-wielding terrorist, who had already killed, emerged from Fishmongers' Hall onto London Bridge and was overcome by a brave individual brandishing a narwhal tusk that he had grabbed from a display in the hall. A city is more than its buildings, and this episode speaks of the City's character. The Renaissance had their cabinets of curiosities, or Wunderkammer (wonder room), where the weird and wonderful were collected for display. London itself is a collection of strange things. The museums, its institutions and its eclectic collection of architecture, people, dress, and customs, is itself a cabinet of curiosities. Some of these curiosities are not without danger. The colonial legacy, including homegrown terrorism, is all around. The peculiar ceremonies of the City's livery companies rival even the Royal Household for pageantry. The dress of the Beefeaters or the Swan Uppers, even the Pearly Kings and Queens, is certainly curious. There is evidence of the appetite among Londoners to keep all this going when you consider that there is now a Worshipful Company of Information Technologists. The Victorians had pilfered the world of interesting and valuable objects. They had an autistic zeal to collect everything from stuffed birds to shrunken heads, and the harm to other cultures and the environment was not a consideration. There is increasing international pressure to begin repatriation of some of these objects. The return of the Elgin Marbles, for example, would be a grand gesture of redemption.

The new London Bridge, replacing a nineteenth-century one sold to an American oil tycoon in 1968, is a dull and practical structure. It was at this point of the river, the furthest point inland where seagoing ships could anchor in the tide, that the Romans built the first crossing in AD 50 in Londinium. and the Port of London was born.

The masterpiece which is The Shard, an epic achievement of ambition and design, stands over 300 metres high on the south bank just east of the bridge. Leaning over towards Dave's kayak, I was telling him about my admiration for this tower. Dave thought it hilarious that it was built by Renzo Piano. 'Renzo's not such an unusual name,' I pointed out.

Tower Bridge, often confused with London Bridge, is another iconic London image. We all assembled alongside the long-anchored HMS Belfast and paddled under the bridge close to the south bank. The bridge has a mechanism which allows tall ships through by raising a central section with carefully balanced counterweights. It is called a bascule bridge.

Up close like this, at the river's level, the view is surprising. The proportions of the bridge are somehow oversized. There is nothing fine or elegant. The towers are thicker than I had expected, and the cables huge. This made the lifted road section seem extremely short. Despite its size, the construction reminds me of a children's toy or a simple automaton. I pictured a giant child kneeling down, crushing all around and operating the system with clumsy soft fists, like in an awful film when the technology for these illusions was new.

The current was still quite slow, and the choppiness was lessening. The drizzle stopped and we saw the sun at last. There was a fair flotilla of jetsam around us. The smell of the river was changing. It had begun with an urban sting, but earthy fields could still be detected. It was now becoming sulphuric and the faint acrid taint of burnt plastic couldn't be missed. I saw Mark's kayak collide heavily with a section of scaffold board and there were assorted plastic cartons and bits of old pallet caught in the eddies just east of the bridge. From here on, downstream was to become the industrial heartland of the City. As trade increased, the wealthy shipping companies began building their own docks ever further eastwards. The last to be built was King George V Dock in 1921. London's docks had been until then the heart of Empire.

There have been at least some craft visible all the time on the river, but there are wharves, piers, bollards, and all manner of evidence all the way through London of maritime activity now long gone. It seems to be an underused resource. Road traffic is so difficult relative to river traffic in London that perhaps this might eventually be revitalised. There are only a handful of commuters using this option and almost no goods delivered by boat. The traditional canal barge delivery of coal, which is slow but with enough barges can deliver a constant stream of coal, like a conveyor belt, might be considered for a variety of goods in constant need in the city.

Onwards towards Docklands there are two big loops in the river. The going was easy. The riverbanks between here and Docklands are crowded with newish apartment buildings all jostling to win the best and closest river view. Any planning care in this is not at all visible. These money-spinning developments, starting from the Thatcherite 1980s, are a visual unacceptable face of capitalism. There is a whiff of greed and corruption.

This is the historic location of the opium dens of Sherlock Holmes, the working bustle in Dickens' stories, the slums and poverty of seafaring visitors, brothels, and taverns.

Now we paddle in equal measure past wealth and privilege; poverty and despair; royalty and ragamuffins. It is a crowded place. Along the banks, among so many, acting out somewhere close will be treachery and loyalty; sadness and success; unrequited love and deep joy. All life goes on as the river's tides breathe in and out in its daily cycle.

We enjoyed the view of Canary Wharf as we made our way slowly with dripping patience. Our wrists let thin streams of cold water under our sleeves. The rowing action means that these water trickles often travel uncomfortably past your armpit and send a chill down your flanks.

London's docks were closing from the 1960s as trade moved to the modern purpose-built docks near the sea. The derelict wasteland left behind has now been transformed into a brave new financial centre.

A sleek commuter river bus quietly sped in front of us, leaving us rocking like see-saws over the wake. Some of us who were not able to face directly to the wake had a close call to capsize. The guide was trying to herd us all close together. We collected in one of those currents on the downstream side of a jetty that create a still spot, where we were drawn back very slowly upstream. We were able to talk together for a while. Nobody was fatigued. Smiles all around. We set off again on the southbound loop of the Isle of Dogs.

We were at Canary Wharf. Dwarfed by sky-reaching steels, our boats such small fry under these armour-clad knights of the top table, as silver as London drizzle. Financial capitals everywhere are populated by ambitious people. Traders are gamblers. They can win in a bull or a bear market. There is little shame here in gaining from the misery of others. In this place, money is the Almighty and the outcome of this worship is modern feudalism. The population of Canary Wharf is swollen daily by numbers equal to those living in a medium-sized town. Small groups of people among these commuters hold sway over vast fortunes and dire impoverishment. Financial disasters rock the world with regularity and affect us all. The world's financial centres are always at work. National boundaries mean little in the convoluted international investment world. Corporations have the power of nations. For some, these catastrophes are like the slow death from a septic bite. Inequality of wealth and opportunity is debated earnestly in the straw-coloured villa upriver, but it only seems to increase as the wealth of those running the giant corporations and banks grows exponentially. Serfdom is still with us.

We ran the final furlong onto the concrete standing just beyond the Cutty Sark. We were relieved of our kayaks, spray decks and buoyancy equipment and, unusually for us, we had no responsibility for them from there on. This was peculiarly freeing. We all headed, bedraggled and happy, to a large pub on the river, which had given permission for us to change in the toilets. We all made a great noise and commotion ripping off sodden wear, and dried off, to collect at the bar for a debriefing over beer and chips.

CHAPTER 7

PEMBROKESHIRE COAST

Movement, movement everywhere: blink an eye and the world is changed

We had met up at Easter for tea and cakes to discuss our next week together on the water, and reflecting on the seagoing parts of our Scottish trip, we settled on devising a route along the Pembrokeshire coast. We allowed a two-week window to delay departure if we needed as we carefully monitored wind conditions to maximise our chances of fair weather. Headwind at sea is a spoiler. We set off on a fine day in late September, bedding down for our first night in sand dunes at Penally Beach just west of Tenby.

Only the Forestry Commission owns more land in the UK than the Ministry of Defence (MOD) and many miles of coastline along our intended route include MOD property at the Castlemartin ranges, Merrion Training Camp, ranges at Manorbier and a training camp here at Penally. Across our heavily populated small country, MOD lands have retained restricted access to vehicles and people, ironically allowing the dark arts of warfare to help preserve nature from the ravages of modern farming practices and urban development.

We had parked our truck in the car park of the tiny Penally railway station. We packed up most of our equipment in the double and single kayak and hauled the boats through the hand-operated white iron rail crossing gates, and then took a few journeys back and forth to the beach several hundred metres away, crossing Penally Range. Mark is like my spaniel; although he takes short paces, he's always running ahead or diverting up and down side banks to survey our position in tireless continual movement, muttering as he goes like Alice's white rabbit. He does more miles to the mile than most of us. The sun was low but warm. Long shadows followed us, undulating and bobbing along the gorse-lined sandy tracks. It was hot work and shirts were off. Dave waved goodbye to Ivor the Engine behind us. An evening dog walker stopped to chat. 'You're all a bit old for this sort of caper,' he said, when we'd told him our plans. In the following days, Dave made many attempts to repeat this in his poorly executed accent that sounded more Indian than Welsh.

We had decided on open-air camping for the trip, in part to save space and weight, but tonight, no tent was no issue; it was a soft sandy bed on a warm night. The beach is protected from the prevailing wind by Giltar Point, a narrow promontory that fingers its way out to sea in front and to the right or west of our

PEMBROK[E]

FINISH St David's

10-mile day

Brawdy

13th–20th 2019

Solva
Newgale
Nolton Haven

St Brides Bay

11-mile day

St Brides

Broad Haven
Little Haven
Sandy Haven

Atlantic Ocean

4-mile day

Skomer

Marloes
Dale

Milford Haven

⛺ CAMP
🏰 CASTLE

St Annes Head

SCOFF!

ESHIRE
COAST
SEPTEMBER
39 MILES
NI
I
E
W
F
SEAL
YEE! HAA!
PEMBROKE
NEYLAND
PEMBROKE DOCK
PEMBROKE
START
TENBY
PENALLY
FRESHWATER EAST
MANORBIER
STACKPOLE
BOSHERTON
14-mile day
BROADHAVEN SOUTH
N
W
E
S
2
4
6
8
MILES
Dave Chisholm FRGS

nest. As dark fell, an oystercatcher screamed, the echo looming and receding in perfect Doppler effect as it traversed the shoreline. Behind us in the scrub, a dunnock in the dunes trilled at the gleaming stars.

✂

We were up at dawn. At this time of year, the sun rises just before seven o'clock, so by the time we had packed and eaten, it was eight o'clock before we launched, splashing and spluttering from grounded kayaks till they lifted and floated comfortably into the choppy sea.

I am the weakest link of the three of us with seagoing paddling because I can suffer from seasickness. I was continually going over in my mind how I would deal with any sickness, and I felt trepidation, unable to resign myself to acceptance of my fate if things went wrong. I had taken Hyoscine tablets to help, wore acupressure wrist bands and kept a large chunk of raw ginger in my pocket. My mouth was already stinging with the sharp tang of ginger, and I held a lump of ginger skin in my cheek to fall back on. Of the three defences, I have found raw ginger to be most effective. It also seems to help if I concentrate on the horizon. I was determined to reduce my risk of spoiling our adventure.

Mark had now purchased his own single kayak and its cockpit was a bit tight for Dave and me, so we took my stout double together. As we pushed on past the breaking surf, Mark looked over to us and shouted encouragement. The wind was over 12 mph, which is only referred to as a moderate breeze, but I was anxiously watching the wave size increase as we headed towards Giltar Point. It was an easterly tide current but a westerly wind, so with wind over tide, we had a pro and an against-good progress. We had known that today would offer these conditions and we were aware that our first challenge was to be an onset of swell as we rounded the headland. We would meet this within half an hour. I was not especially concerned for our safety, although a capsize would be a struggle. We had practised recovery many times, and Mark in his single could probably simply roll back up. It was the possibility of sickness that frightened me.

I had warned the boys of this, but I had managed a trouble-free forty miles or so of open sea in Scotland, and they seemed confident that I would be fine. I had been the safety escort kayak on one of Dave's Kingsdown Crawlers' sea swim jaunts from St Margaret's to Deal, and there had to be many still periods, as the swimmers are slow, the kayak left bobbing up and down in the swell. I had been sick at sea, struggling to endure the whole route, then after landing it had taken five or six miserable days before the nausea finally left. I was not as confident as my mates that I would manage.

We were soon saturated, but the early progress and salty spray was exhilarating. Both sun and sea were warm. Looking behind and right to land, it was surprising how far from land we had quickly paddled. The waves began lifting us up and down in greater degrees as the swell became larger as we rounded Giltar Point. We couldn't always keep the bow directly into the wave direction, and we were gradually getting used to the required body movements to counter all this, like a bird keeping its head completely still as the wire it perches upon swings to and fro. This required a lot of concentration. I began to forget about being sick.

Mark looked at ease in his kayak. He paddled up close and we were able to discuss identifying our location. He had laminated a map of each projected day's paddle, which we had strapped under the netting in front of each cockpit. We were halfway between the mainland and Caldey Island, which was slightly behind us now. The next spit of land was clearly visible a few miles ahead, close to Lydstep.

We counted the headlands off one by one, and paddled on in similar conditions for ten miles. The shoreline became hazy as the afternoon approached. We were about a mile out to sea. I thought about my condition and was aware of a little dizzy discomfort but had confidence I would survive this. Much bigger seas and we wouldn't be going out, so if I was OK today, I'd probably make the grade. We hadn't planned where to break up the day, but we decided it was time for a snack and a rest, so we pulled up after the next headland, which led us onto the flat sandy beach at Freshwater East. The bay is sheltered, and as we approached the shore, the waves were long and shallow. We headed in at a right angle to the waves, paddling hard to achieve a surf ride with raised stern, right onto the beach. We clambered out into a few inches of warm water, smacked a high-five and watched Mark follow our lead, racing onto the sand.

The beach was empty of people. We stretched and walked circulation back into our legs. It was cool and a gentle breeze kept the atmosphere fresh. Bright sun came and went between huge white clouds that made stately progress, rolling and merging above. While we revived with hot tea and chat, we decided upon one more break in the day before a final stop at Broad Haven South Beach for the night. We had researched the leg after this and it was time critical because we had to pass the live firing range at Castlemartin on a Sunday when it was permitted. The weather calmed a little in the afternoon. After our second stop at Barafundle Bay, we were setting off onto a flat sea, deep blue and occasionally glinting and winking at us reassuringly. The double, with two of us powering the propulsion is a little faster, but Mark in his single was continually paddling up close, then falling back or racing ahead. We were relaxed and becoming accustomed to the movements and counter-movements to stay steady.

The beach at Broad Haven is a sandy scallop lying between rocky cliffs. There is a distinctive rock formation, known as Church Rock, that lies a few hundred metres out to sea in the middle of the bay. Later that night, we would see the sun setting immediately behind this, creating the silhouette of what, unsurprisingly, appeared like a church. After we had landed, we quickly laid out our boats on the far western side of the beach, where we found a convenient indent in the craggy cliff with soft sand above the high-tide mark and useful ledges and rocks to spread out our equipment and clothes to dry.

Plenty of daylight remained, and we knew about vast lily ponds behind the beach on the unoccupied Stackpole Estate. Dave stayed with the boats, and Mark and I set off to find them. We trotted off across the warm sand towards a shallow stream flowing over the beach and followed the stream inland. We climbed a gentle rise towards a small bridge and we found the route that Mark had identified on the map. The sudden change from sand and open beach to soft soil and dense tree canopy was remarkable. The map shows a sort of Neptune's trident-shaped waterway extending inland. We followed the dappled path along the eastern prong. We seemed to emerge from undergrowth into an open area to unexpectedly view the stunning scene of thousands of white lilies floating for as far as we could see, populating most of the surface of the broad and sinuous lake. Thinking of the Nile Delta, I told Mark that we should be careful of crocodiles. Mark stood very upright, shielding his eyes from the sun. I could see that he too was taken aback at the sight in front of us. 'Good Lord,' is all he said.

We followed a signed path that more or less circumnavigates the lily ponds. The Campbells, earls of Cawdor, created this scene from 1760. Strangely, we had explored some of the lands of that privileged family when we were kayaking along the Firth of Forth. Here, the family followed the eighteenth-century fashion of creating ambitious romantic landscapes by building weirs across three adjacent valleys, slowing the streams as they approached the sea and creating this spectacular feature, usually referred to as Bosherton Lily Ponds.

The National Trust are now stewards of the estate, but along our way, we noticed the decayed elegance of stone relics, follies, bridges, and old walls. The Devil's Quoit, an ancient standing stone on our path, has looked out over the windswept cliffs for five thousand years. The stone is set at the high point in a meadow next to the path, and today, there was a profusion of common blue butterflies, downy and drowsy, flitting about the tussocky grass. We paused on the eight-span stone bridge across the pond, and watched shoals of roach through gaps in the lilies. A heron wrestled with a fish that promptly disappeared in one gulp down its narrow neck. The evening had become still, and away from the sea, it was warm. We walked at a fair pace, with Mark scampering his trademark diversions here and there. I pointed out a tree creeper that was on its own circumnavigation of a grizzly old oak trunk.

On the western prong of the trident, I persuaded Mark to sit and enjoy the peace of the dying day. We sat on beech roots, looking through towards the ponds and were gratified to watch a spotted flycatcher that made the same flight path again and again from its perch on an alder branch overhanging the lake, acrobatically seizing insect prey and returning to eat each time on the same perch. Dragonflies were everywhere, patrolling like drones. Crickets trilled constantly like a kitten's purr.

We could see that sections of this part of the ponds had silted up, and wetlands of reed and willow had taken over, offering a different kind of home to wildlife. There were warblers and buntings, frogs, and kingfishers. The area is also home to otters. The topography and history of the immediate area has saved the ponds from the damaging effect of nitrogen enrichment from agricultural runoff. We had seen the subsequent deoxygenation and algal blooms this can cause in tributaries of the River Wye.

These ponds are colonised by what are called stonewort meadows: submerged tracts of land where these plants have spread successfully. We could see the plants everywhere, like a forest understory. There are thirty-three species of stonewort (charophytes) in Britain, and I was aware of the importance of these plants. I am familiar with the Little Stour Valley near my home, which is known to be a place where stonewort varieties thrive. Bosherton Ponds, however, are in a different league of abundance, both in volume and variety of species. Stoneworts are a unique group of algae that grow in fresh or brackish water. If seaweed, also algae, dominates the botanical world of the sea, then stoneworts are the masters of freshwater. Of the many peculiarities of this species, two are that it has, at 20 centimetres long, the largest cells known to science; and second, they build an encrusted external skeleton from calcium carbonate instead of using cellulose for structural support. If you handle stonewort, you will be surprised that the feel of the plant, which at a glance looks like an ordinary flowering plant, is nodular, rough, and brittle. The limestone substrate in this area provides the hard water and calcium required. The chemistry behind this process is apparently complex, but the build-up is like the furring of a kettle. They thrive where nutrients are low, and they are unable to tolerate significant levels of phosphates or nitrates, so they are excellent indicators of nutrient pollution and water quality. They are the canaries of our freshwater.

We completed our circuit, returning to Dave and the boats as dusk deepened. We were pleased with early progress and we sat up chatting on the sand. I'm always the first in bed and I stretched out listening to hushed voices and gentle laughter. It was dry but quite cold. We planned for a very early start in the morning to make sure that we had the tidal currents with us and were able to comfortably cross the MOD-controlled coastal route on the Sunday when it is permitted. This was not to go to plan at all.

※

It was before daybreak that Dave called over to me that we should start looking lively and begin packing up. I had had a fitful night and was already awake. I had a problem. My heartbeat was irregular and felt like it was flip-flopping from side to side. This had been with me for a couple of hours. It was not just passing palpitations. I had recently been under doctor's surveillance for occasional symptoms of atrial fibrillation. It was unfamiliar and uncomfortable. I had to tell Dave and Mark that I needed to sit this out. I felt the stress of letting the side down, worrying that the trip might have to be abandoned, with a little irony that I was, after all, surviving possible seasickness. I hadn't learned much about the condition, but in the past, it had always disappeared within an hour. I slowly dressed and sat up against the rocks. Things were not improving and I couldn't possibly set off to sea. I decided to try to see a doctor.

The boys were concerned. They spoke softly and gave me space, both physically and mentally, to assess the situation. I tried to reassure them that it would pass. We discussed our options and it was agreed that I would make my way to a hospital, ideally by ambulance, leaving them on the beach with the boats. Mark helped me slowly up the long walk of steep steps to the top of the cliff where we could see there was a car park. I was hoping for mobile phone reception.

I got through to the ambulance service. They told me that I needed to make my own way to the hospital in Pembroke. A slight, grey-haired woman was the only other person in the car park. She had at least partly overheard my conversation and offered to take me most of the way in her car, and I could call a taxi for the remaining distance. Mark, standing with his hand on his hip, bottom lip wrapped over his top one and raised eyebrows in a sympathetic look of well-wishing, waved me off before turning back to the beach.

The kindly old lady told me that she'd had the same health problem when she lived in London, but when her husband had died five years ago, she had sold up and moved here, in bucolic bliss, quite near the beach. She told me that her lifestyle change had cured her, and she was now completely free of her past problems. She said that she was known locally as the 'beach lady' because she swam at this beach every day, all year round. She sounded calm and projected a tenderness that made me feel relaxed and sleepy as she manoeuvred her way around the small, sunken lanes with mossy drystone wall borders.

I was dropped off at the church of St Gwynog's in St Twynnells, called a taxi and was soon in a hospital waiting room. The wait was lengthy and I dozed off briefly. When I awoke on the NHS orange vinyl seating, I could immediately feel that my heartbeat had returned to normal. A doctor eventually checked me over and assured me that I could return to activities with no restrictions. I have since educated myself further on the condition and have undergone a corrective procedure that seems to have been successful. I was back with my paddling partners by early afternoon.

The beach was now dotted with strollers and bathers. The sun and the sand were warm. We huddled together around our brightly coloured kayaks to discuss our plan. Mark was immediately good to continue but Dave, who after all was in my kayak, needed convincing that it was responsible to continue. We all quickly agreed to press on. We had missed our chance to continue past the firing ranges to the west, so it was decided that I would taxi back to Tenby in the morning to collect the truck, and we would then drive the following leg to Martin's Haven at the southern end of St Brides Bay. This would also give me a day of rest as a precaution. There was a pub near the top of the cliffs and I decided to increase my chances of good recovery by sleeping there that evening in a proper bed.

By late afternoon, we had all been in the sea for a swim. Dave, with the comfortable crawl-breathing technique of a seasoned swimmer, seems to glide along effortlessly with rhythmic rolling body, balanced easy arm action and regular disturbance at his feet like the propeller froth of a small boat. Mark and I splashed around in the shallows like children. The beach was again empty. As we took the long walk along the flat sand where the tide had withdrawn, we were surprised to see a stream of visitors making their way speedily down the zig-zag steps to the beach. There were maybe fifty of them. All were fit-looking young men and they streamed onto the beach as Dave too made his exit from the water.

Within fifteen minutes, all shirts were off, a football pitch had been laid out, and a series of tables and catering-scale barbecue equipment had been set in a line, just a few metres from our kayak camp. Rows of steaks were soon being grilled on the fire. The unmistakable waft of charred protein drifted appetisingly amid billows of white smoke. The hiss and spit drew our attention and we looked at each other like dogs at a dinner bowl. Plates were placed alongside salads. Rice and potatoes were piled up. Frantic activity came from the football. Athletic limbs flailed about. Jostling and challenging were good humoured and accompanied by yelling and laughing.

One of the cooks of this party walked over to us. He had short black hair, an upright demeanour, and the lanky look of youth yet to fully bloom. He spoke in a stiff but courteous manner. We had already guessed that this might be a military presence and we were correct. This was Sunday evening at the beach for a platoon from the Royal Tank Regiment on exercises at Castlemartin. He asked us to help ourselves to their supper. We said that we would pass on the football but would really appreciate joining them for a feed. We spent an hour eating and chatting in the company of these polite young men. These are the souls who are consumed in conflict around the world, yet here we were, drinking beer and eating steak on a sunny Sunday afternoon on a sandy haven. The lads here, not long from maybe listening to music in their untidy bedrooms with Mum and Dad downstairs and younger sister in the next room, would be little different from the young men and women in tank platoons from Ukraine, Russia, or Israel.

After the party had left the beach, speedily with efficiency, after a couple of hours there was no evidence that they had ever been here apart from footprints in the sand. Our enclave returned to us alone as the sun again slid behind Castle Rock. The lullaby of tiny lapping waves pushed bubbly sheets of effervescent white foam over the flat shiny foreshore. The distant melancholic cries of gulls echoed around the red cliffs.

※

A cab took me in the morning back to the station car park at Penally. By the time I was back at Broadhaven South, the boys had carried everything, including the boats, up the long and steep steps to the National Trust car park. My skiving didn't go without comment.

Now with a vehicle we stopped for some of the tourist sights on our way to St Brides Bay. Nearby was the six-acre walled garden of the Stackpole Estate, which once grew pineapples and all necessary fruit and vegetables to service the tables of the Campbell family at Stackpole Court. We sauntered around the garden, helping ourselves to fruits from heavily laden trees. Now the garden is owned by the National Trust, with Mencap offering adults with learning disabilities the opportunity of horticultural experience. The military that we had encountered on the beach played some role in the demise of the estate and the great house known as Stackpole Court. The MOD requisitioned 6,000 acres, half the estate, in the build-up to the Second World War, to create the Castlemartin Firing Range. This, along with the expense needed to run the place, made it financially unviable. Soldiers were billeted at the huge house, and it is said that much of the roof lead was stripped and sold by the temporary occupants, which allowed the weather to begin the cycle of destructive dry rot. The Campbells gave up on the old pile at the end of the war and it was finally pulled down in 1963.

We made our way to Pembroke. The town has some charm, and we had fun crawling over the ramparts of Pembroke Castle. Dave had a particular interest in some of the exhibits because of his cartoon work. In addition to twenty-five years' work on *The Sunday Times*, he has also been involved with numerous landmark and museum cartoons. We spent a couple of hours educating ourselves on Welsh history. The industrial feel of the area outside the castle environs in the adjacent Pembroke Dock is in stark contrast to the beauty of the crystal-clear spring-fed, lily-clad waters of Bosherton or the stately fallen elegance of Stackpole. The area has a feel of a 1970s working men's club, before a refit, with graffiti, drugs, and poverty.

Late in the day, we drove on to the Marloes peninsula. That evening, at a pub close to where we planned to stay near Skomer Island, we tried to glean some local information on the best time and tide to paddle across to, and possibly around, the island. The island is less than a mile off shore, but we knew that tides at certain times meant very strong currents and we needed to time our crossing safely. We had overheard a stout blond mop-haired youngish man at the bar. His loud conversation made us realise that he had a fishing boat. He would surely be our man. Dave approached him, offered to buy him a pint, expecting the generosity of spirit often received from strangers when you ask for help. As soon as Dave said the word 'kayak', his brow blackened. His advice to us was 'Don't go'.

'I'm fed up with rescuing you fuckers!' he yelled, now sounding drunk. Mark and I chipped in and we did our best to overcome his aggression with charm and reason. Like most travellers and adventurers, we liked to think that we were somehow better than tourists, but tourists we were. Pembrokeshire has a fair overdose of visitors from England. Kayaking in the sea is popular here. The local economy might rely on us tourists, but the local dichotomy, often evident in honeypot destinations of need, around the distaste of busy roads, high house prices and general disruption to life, was venting robustly through our Welsh fisherman. We calmed him down in the end and we did at least receive one piece of useful information: 'If you have to go, don't go tomorrow, there will be a strong swell. Forecast is better later in the week.'

We immediately decided to progress north around St Brides Bay towards St Davids for the next two days then return here on our last day to cross Broad Sound and explore Skomer Island. We offloaded all our equipment at the top of a steep path to the sheltered cove from where the tiny Skomer ferry operates, and I drove to a nearby farm that agreed to let me park for a few days. I walked back. It was windy with some rain. We all backed up against a drystone wall in our bivvy bags to shelter from the sea wind. Two days out of the sea had given my head a chance to stop wallowing in waves. I slept well.

CHAPTER 7 — PEMBROKESHIRE COAST

※

The drunken fisherman was correct. In the morning the sea was choppy, and a fair wind was gusting persistently. We could see swirling currents as the water flattened in the narrows between the mainland and the island. We knew that the tide was receding, which meant a southerly flow and we were to head north, so we expected some tough paddling.

Tottering down the rocky path to the beach was a chilly experience, but at least it wasn't raining. We all had bare legs and looked top-heavy with our buoyancy aids over our shoulders and spray skirts about our waists. I could see spiky hairs and goosebumps on Dave's legs in front of me, silhouetted against the glare from the sea.

It was tricky pushing out over the breaking waves close to shore, but once a hundred metres out to sea, it was not as difficult as we had feared. We were paddling against the wind and against the tide. Wind blew spray in our faces and the cold water dripped down the paddles and up our sleeves. The waves were occasionally five or six feet and we had to concentrate the whole time. Mark grinned with unnecessary glee. He was confident and enjoying the challenge. Dave and I in the double had a disadvantage, having to account for the other's movements to balance. I was feeling an edge of anxiety but was able to tell myself that the worst that could happen wasn't so bad. We weren't far out to sea and we knew what to do if we capsized. It was difficult to chat to Dave in the front of the boat, and I had to yell to be heard, but I did try. I'd taken to calling Dave 'the fisherman's friend', and I reminded him: 'I'm fed up with rescuing you fuckers,' It was easier to talk across the water to Mark. We kept a close formation. After an hour's hard going, we came into the lee of a headland. The wind eased, the swell dropped and even the sun appeared.

The shore was now all red sandstone cliffs. It was reminiscent of the cliffs in the middle Wye. The putty-grey-coloured limestone had gone. We paddled close to shore and decided on an early break and a chance to land where only low tide exposes the beach under the rugged cliffs. Few people would have the chance to visit these areas because kayak access is one of the few safe ways to land.

We selected a narrow slither of sand along the base of the cliffs. The beach approach was shallow and landing was easy. We hauled the boats onto the exposed wet sand. It was completely sheltered and the sun shone directly at us over the bay. It was like a secret world. It was as if we had discovered a new continent. The cliffs were full of life. Life not usually seen on land. Huge ravens croaked from ledges and wheeled above us, their livery glistening jet black. Several hundred metres away on the same beach, we could see a group of grey seals moving only slightly, like maggots in a bait box. There were guillemots now visible on the water. To one side a cacophony of kittiwakes squabbled like children on a long car journey, the rocks below had ledges all stained white by guano. Mark was the first to see choughs and he pointed excitedly and we could clearly see the telltale curved bright red beak. Both ravens and choughs were once a common site across Britain. These birds have survived here and we were later to see a hooded crow to add to our corvid count. Mark had already trotted in his quick-step fashion up and down the beach while Dave and I gawped in wonder at our new land. Mark was now looking down and not up. He squatted and called us over. He had found otter tracks – loads of them in the wet sand. We were never to see an otter, but at least we knew they were here.

My imagination now coloured by the discovery of a distant and forgotten land once back at sea, the water seemed a richer colour than ever. At times it glowed mysteriously with the deepest indigo. A different view, or change in current, saw hues of grey, green, turquoise, and even streaks of ephemeral violet. The air around us seemed cleaner than ever. The iodine sting in our nostrils had the scent of cleansing a wound. Healing and regeneration of spirit flowed from within. My companions seemed closer than ever, trustworthy, and warm. We were sharing something hard to find. This was precious. A euphoria buoyed our progress.

Travelling as we were, slowly and stutteringly, you notice that while you may be observing the nature around you, the wildlife is also observing you. There is interaction all the time. It's not at all like reading about nature or watching TV from a remote protected environment. You are part of it, within it. A bird flies off in response to your movement. Sometimes eye contact is made, acknowledging your presence. The responses are intimate and quick. The feel of the water or the wind, the smells, and the sounds all interact. You feel a belonging to a larger world. I had always thought that these times allowed you to park up problems and be free of life's burdens, but it's a greater benefit than that. It enables you to simply accept how things are. Many things in your life will always be beyond your control, so you may as well just go along with them, like the flow of a river or the turning of the tide.

I threw out a line with a feather on the hook to trawl behind us. This was then forgotten as we paddled further out around the headland. Thankfully the wind was receding and the swell had become manageable. The tide was on the turn now, so the current would soon be in our favour. Mark came alongside and Dave held his kayak while Mark looked closely at the laminated map on his deck. We could make a straight line towards St Brides Haven, cutting off distance by avoiding shore hugging. We deemed the weather suitable for this. Visibility was excellent and we could easily identify landmarks on shore.

Approaching the tiny secluded bay that is St Brides Haven, the water became shallow and as clear as tap water. A Liquorice Allsorts array of smooth coloured rocks dotted the sandy seabed, the sunlight through the water magnifying their form like a lava lamp, glooping and bulging as we drifted over them. We slowed to remove a floating plastic sack, only to discover that we were alongside a basketball-sized jellyfish, with a lace-like purple rim at the fringe of a creamy domed head. It trailed eight raggedy arms flowing half a metre behind. Dave is the jellyfish identifier among us because they are a possible hazard in his open-water exploits. He told us that this was a barrel jellyfish, harmless, but also the largest in UK waters. The profusion of all the fish-eating creatures that we encountered, both bird and beast, must mean that fish stocks were good. Before landing, I pulled in my line to find that I had caught a small cod. 'I know all about catching fish,' I crowed.

The tiny beach had a picnic table set up just above the sand and pebble beach. We immediately set about drying what we could over the pebbles. After brewing tea,

I made the mistake of trying to fry my pathetic catch without oil. We managed to savour a morsel each from the black skin stuck to the pan. It was like all sitting down to feast on a cockle.

Mark was scampering about while Dave and I plotted the remaining day's journey. We planned to finish the day at Druidston Haven, a few miles north and a mid-point of St Brides Bay.

We knew that the tide would assist us for only another hour, so we tried to make the best of that advantage and set off at a brisk paddle. The sun was warm when not concealed, but the wind again began to gust head on, and the swell was increasing. The course had few promontories or headlands to shelter us and we kept a course, heads down, just a hundred metres off shore. Gulls reeled and cried above. We saw the bobbing heads of grey seals all the time. Cormorants flew low above the choppy sea, and we saw many more of the barrel jellyfish on this section. It was late afternoon by the time we pulled our boats up for the day on the sand and pebbles at Druidston.

We identified a suitable slightly sheltered part of the beach to establish ourselves for the night. We forayed the area. There was a small watercourse making its way through a break in the cliffs with grassy sand dunes leading back to farmland. There were well-worn paths down to our beach from here, but for now, the beach was our own. We thought that a fire was not appropriate. We had head torches and a tiny gas cooker. That evening, it was Mark who took on the cooking. He busied himself unpacking and packing dry bags until he had all his ingredients together. Living out of a few bags that have to be forever accessed and rearranged means that you are always trying to keep things tidy and in place. Mark is excellent at this. Once you can't find something, the frustration is tedious. It is usually Dave or me that ends up pulling the entrails out of our dry bags again and again, accompanied by some choice expletives.

The pebbles were deep and averaging at chicken's-egg size so were just small enough that we could each create a kind of hollowed out bed made comfortable by the cushion of our sleeping mats. The weather was again kind. It was cool but thankfully dry and very clear. The prominent rocks were used to drape over and dry our equipment. A kind of homemaking ownership emerges when we settle down. You might return to a particular ledge where you'd put down your toothpaste or whatever, and that ledge becomes yours. The others couldn't possibly consider intruding with their own stuff. An intimate familiarity emerges with the makeshift home of the nomad. The feel and use of every feature quickly becomes known. The ownership in our coterie of temporary itinerants is fed by sincere courtesy. There is no pecking order and it's not even first come first served regarding, for instance, who bags the most level sleeping patch. An ownership is established and remains until everything is stowed in the boats and the camp vacated.

As dusk turned to dark, a murmuration of starlings shimmied like a vast shoal of fish, shaping and reforming, reminding me of the submerged rocks at St Brides Haven, distorting like a lava lamp. They finally settled, noisily establishing their own temporary camp, roosting in trees beyond the beach. A distant siren cry of grey seals wailing carried across the flat sand in front of the pebble beach, echoing around the cliffs. Eventually I was lying flat, staring into the cool night sky; Dave's familiar night-time wailing answered the seals' persistent pleas. I bundled the covers over my head and my breathing warmed the sleeping bag. I wondered what the seals were thinking.

✕

We wanted to reach Porthclais at St Davids by late afternoon on our penultimate day. The tide would be with us for the morning at least, so we were on the water before seven am. We were again lucky with the weather. The slight wind was behind us. The coast continued with rugged black-red cliffs, caves, rocks and swirling pools, all full of life. Our paddles dunking in and out of the clear water gained rhythm. The inky hues of the sea shifted and merged with the variations in depth, the wind on the surface and the currents below. We didn't talk. We were feeling life moment by moment. The familiar march of our journey brought on a hypnotising autopilot and the day slowly began to spill its contents onto our waking senses.

Coal mining has dominated South Wales industry for the previous two centuries and the coal fields extended as far west as this central section of the bay. We could see spoil heaps of open cast mining fully grassed over and peaceful as we rounded the distinctive landmark known as Rickets Head at Nolton Haven. The geological headland feature is a standing column of sandstone, and from where we were viewing it, the sea appeared like a giant thumbs-up, which I took to be approval and encouragement from the gods.

Stretching in front of us now was a two-mile stretch of flat ash-blond beach. This is Newgale Sands. The beach is a well-known surfers' haunt, so traversing along the beach, we needed to do what we could to reduce side-on wave encounters. It was fresh but without strong winds. The waves were persistent and rolling in groups towards the mainland, but they were small enough to safely tackle in our fully laden boats. We stayed far enough out to avoid the breaking surf, until we headed straight in at the far end of the bay, racing a joyride with the frothy surf to the shell-studded sand flats.

It was only just past eight in the morning. Stripping off our wet gear, having already completed a leg of the day's paddling, with the chilly dripping of water on our limbs, it felt slightly wrong. 'You should always do some work before breakfast,' I said, as if this was normal for me.

The small village sits gratefully behind a huge pebble bank, created by a storm in 1857, that now acts as a natural sea defence and runs the whole distance behind the beach. The place has a gentle seaside holiday feel to it, with surfboards, kayaks and bodyboards for hire. There are faded ice cream signs and small shops with flip-flops, fluttering plastic, and tinsel paraphernalia. We returned to sea, full of hot tea and calories from an unhealthy breakfast.

I imagine the shape of Wales to be like a pig's head. St Brides Bay is the nostrils of its rooting snout. This concave nose reaches out into the Atlantic Ocean with its access to the warm waters from the Gulf Stream, direct from the West Indies. And it attracts a rich concoction of fish, squid and plankton being positioned with the geography and undersea topography that cause the strong tidal currents to circulate these nutritious ingredients into a gourmet feast for impressive creatures, other than my Welsh boar, to feed upon. The variety of large marine mammals and fish here is very impressive. The largest is the basking shark, a regular summer visitor, the weight and size of a double-decker bus. If you are lucky, you can see bottlenose, common, and Risso's dolphins; harbour porpoises; minke, sei, and fin whales; loggerhead turtles; many different species of shark; the bizarre-looking sunfish, and even the occasional orca.

We anticipated reaching the harbour village of Solva by midday. We were aware that disturbances to the seal population should be avoided, so we tried to keep this in mind along the following few miles of cliffs and crevices as we made several ventures into inlets and caves. I followed Mark into one deep cave more like a narrow tunnel into the rocks. We could see the dappled seabed through the clear water. Tangles of red and bottle-green seaweed adorned the sides of the vertical, irregular rocks. The walls of the cave shimmied in the reflected sunlight and were largely built of huge three-sided rocks. Despite the strata of sedimentary rock, this appearance gave the impression of crystalline growth. Unexpectedly, we heard the loud moaning of seals just ahead and a large plopping splash. A silky fat seal quickly made its way underneath us to open water, its large black eyes looking up at us as it swam. We couldn't turn our kayaks but reversed out in case there were pups and other seals further down in the recesses of the cave.

Cormorants were by now basking on rocks in the sun, their wings spread open in the familiar crucifix form they favour to dry their wings. We watched choughs spiralling on the cliffs, razorbills, and many guillemots in the sea. A guillemot can dive up to 180 metres in depth and is a record holder for this. Gannets have been a common sight, and we had a very close encounter, every marking on its remarkably streamlined form visible as it plunged like a javelin into the water a few metres from Dave's kayak. Close up, it is surprising how big they are. They have the stocky neck of a boxer, an athletic-looking body, a six-foot wingspan, and a face that looks like Batman's Joker. We were close to Grassholme Island, where ten percent of the entire world's population of northern gannet nest each year.

We entered the lee of a tranquil cove. The undercurrent caused flat areas to appear on the surface of the water in ever-changing fluid movement. The sea colour changed to a milky turquoise. Great twisting paths across the sea appeared between the flat areas. The strata of the rufous rock formations on the cliffs behind echoed this look, like the loops and whorls of a fingerprint. The sky then led upwards, and the purity of colour increased the higher we looked, with wind-blown clouds displaying beautiful calligraphic shapes in extravagant gestures, like the sweeping movement of a dance. It felt as if we were being led into a welcoming embrace.

All around us evoked movement. Some of these forms were graceful and others were staccato and splintered, like the shattered, crumbled ends of rock. Some showed circularity of repose and others whispered delicate, quiet notes. These organic forms can often be described in musical terms, and music is often described in terms of structure and form. If some people can have perfect pitch, so too can some people resonate perfectly with these natural shapes and have perfect pitch in their visual interpretation of nature. This is most evident when working in three dimensions. Great sculptors all have a deep understanding of Nature's language. In the built environment, it was Frank Lloyd Wright who first coined the term 'organic architecture', but the Gothic styles, the potential energy present in the sprung musculature of art nouveau buildings, or more recently in the astonishing work of Zaha Hadid, and others, all show a fundamental understanding of the beauty of natural form.

I've spent much of my life working with so-called 'faux finishes'. This craft is rooted in tradition almost as old as any application of paint to any substrate. I paint surfaces to look like expensive natural materials. These decorative finishes might include elaborately grained or exotic timbers, all manner of stone and marble, sky ceilings, woodland murals and so on. I have often had to match an existing true surface, and sometimes I've created the appearance required completely from within my imagination. I have also had a brief past life as a portrait sculptor. To produce these things, you must observe very closely and reproduce very carefully. Modelling, for example, the labyrinthine folds of a human ear takes patience and clarity of thought. If it is slightly wrong, it is obvious. A portrait that has little resemblance to the sitter is of no value. (I'm in awe of anyone who can carve such things; clay affords you many attempts by contrast.) Over time, you begin to recognise the same patterns, the way natural structure stretches and folds, the way it fragments, the way it repeats and is interrupted. You begin to understand certain rules of growth and movement that apply to all organic form. Mathematicians throughout history, not only the more obvious examples like Fibonacci or Leonardo Da Vinci but modern academics all over the world, try to demonstrate that mathematics is a fundamental part of nature. Their intellect is beyond me, but I have by default picked up, by experience and consequent intuition, some of the rules of natural form and where the most inspiring aspects are to be found. Movement is key to this. How your eye is drawn at different speeds over different forms, and how it settles at certain points is all to be considered in the understanding of composition. Colour can appear to come forward or recede. All nature and all things are in constant movement. Even the geology of rock cliffs is in movement, and all growth is movement. All form in some way reflects this dynamic, whether this is the arching forms of the gannet's wing, the tiny bubbling breaks in the smooth watery paths in front of us, the generous curves of the rock face, or the stuttering repetition of atmospheric waves in cirrocumulus cloud formations. Movement, movement, everywhere: blink an eye and the world is changed.

Artists, writers, and musicians all frequently herald nature as vital to their work in creative expression. This applies also to the decorative arts, applied arts, architecture, ceramics, photography, film, poetry, drama, folklore, product design, and engineering. Nature's influence touches on almost all human activity. If we are aware of this and connect with nature more often, then we may take more care to preserve what we still have, and spend more time in the empathic appreciation and understanding of the natural world around us. We can all learn to read nature's calligraphy. You don't have to be a tree hugger or a romantic poet to embrace the ecstasy of nature's mysticism.

We were all suffering from some fatigue and Dave was suffering from the chaffing seawater legs that can happen below deck, so it was a welcome break when we joined the few late season tourists in the tea shops of Solva. The village and harbour are well known for the crab and lobster caught in the bay and landed here. The visitors seemed affluent and the prices reflected this. The area has substantial numbers of second homes. Kensington and Chelsea may be substantial contributors to the local economy in the summer, but I wondered what villagers remain in the winter.

✶

The last section of the day's paddle was in brilliant sunshine. The main sea craft that we had seen so far were tankers way out in the bay, but other kayaks were now beginning to appear. The closer we were to St Davids, the more activity was around us. The occupants of most of the kayaks seemed to be very young. Our laden boats, with deck netting bursting, and maps, bottles of water, discarded outer clothes, bits of rope and all manner of small souvenir shells and driftwood flopping about in the wind at our laps, suddenly felt cumbersome and constrained. These free spirits had their kayak, their paddle and safety hat, and were freewheeling.

Porthclais is a delightful and tiny sheltered inlet harbour, surrounded by steep gorse-filled banks, close to St Davids. The cove has a harbour wall built out near the entrance from the sea and curves backwards to keep the ravages of the Atlantic at bay. I left Mark and Dave at the harbour and walked to where I had phone reception. I called a taxi and was able to collect the truck and return with daylight remaining. We packed the vehicle with the kayaks on top and made our way to the town.

St Davids is a tiny, compact city, Britain's smallest, with a vibrant tourist industry ensuring it maintains a disproportionate line-up of hotels, cafés, and gift shops. This doesn't detract from its charm and it is studded with ancient buildings and monuments. The old buildings and the local sandstone give an atmosphere of gentle confidence. There is a pervading feeling of permanence. Like a magician hiding a passenger jet, we were in the city centre, no bigger than an English rural village square, but the cathedral was nowhere to be seen. We found the enormous purple-stoned edifice nestled inconspicuously in a valley just a minute's walk away. It was shut at this time, but we enjoyed a pleasant amble around the grounds. We watched swifts racing in a screeching vortex that rose and fell around the megalithic cathedral tower as the shadows of the day reached their maximum length. The city is one of the great historic shrines of Christendom, its story reaching beyond the sixth century, when St David chose this far-flung location as the site of a monastery. *Another visit, another time,* I thought.

The weather looked good for our postponed crossing to Skomer in the morning. It was a cheerful journey together back to the south end of the bay and the car park at Martin's Haven for our last day. We were parked and unloading by eleven am. Dave had managed to make contact with the warden on the island. It is an ecologically important site with restricted access, so they insisted on our arriving strictly at the designated landing spot in a sheltered cove on the northeast corner.

We gingerly carried our boats over the steep rocky beach in the sheltered cove to the sea alongside the ferry pontoon, where early summer visitors to the island queue for the chance to spend the day with puffins. As we made our preparations to climb in our boats and set off, two recreational scuba divers were also preparing to enter the water. In all their equipment, with wet suits, flippers, tanks, masks and so on, they were as slow and uncomfortable looking as any other seagoing creature out of the water. We nodded our greetings. 'Boys with their toys,' muttered Dave, as if we were truly any different.

We had timed our one-mile trip to and from the island, across Jack Sound to catch slack tide for each crossing because the tidal currents at other times can be dangerously powerful. It is a famously treacherous body of water for shipping, with numerous reefs and a tidal race of up to six knots. This schedule would allow us five or six hours on the island.

We stayed close together and accounted from the start for the outgoing tidal current by following a route several hundred metres north and into the current, anticipating a drag through the pinch point between the mainland and the island. I felt some nervousness, recalling the miserable Welsh fishermen we had met earlier. The tidal drift was not at all regular and Dave and I in the double felt a few strange tugs from below that derailed our course and twisted the stern. The water resembled a pan of water, just as it begins to boil. Our tiny vessels, however, cut through the very upper surface only and we made safe progress as we approached the small bay from the north.

There were seals everywhere, bobbing in and out close by and basking in the sunshine on the sand and rocks of the bay, their smooth dappled grey coats dotted with pebble-like black-brown markings. We could see the rough-hewn steps in the rock and someone making their way down them to meet us. The rocks by the steps allowed us easy exit. We tied a line to each boat and left them sitting on the water. We were met by the broad white smile on the fresh face of one of the young women researchers on the island. We were led up to a landing on the stairs, which was fenced and deemed suitable for our 'induction'. We had to obey some rules. I followed at the rear, watching the friendly young woman towering over Dave. Mark was dwarfed by her Amazonian stature. We lined up against the fence and we were given instructions about where we could or could not go and what we should do in order to avoid disturbing the wildlife. Many people make the trip in the early summer to see the puffins, which nest all over. The main wildlife value in the island, however, is its home to Manx shearwater. Half of the world's population call this their home.

We set off on the well-worn four-mile circuitous path that would take us the whole way around the small island. A very gratifying four miles it is. Tall cliffs surround the island – everywhere is 60 metres above sea level – so the views, wherever you are, will be downward-looking and extensive. The puffins had by now left the island for open water until the following year's breeding season. The Manx shearwaters, however, as our guide had told us, were now nearing the fledging stage and were here in huge numbers. The adults leave their chicks for the day in their nests, which are deep in burrows, so we were unlikely to see them in daylight hours.

The treeless landscape, largely of rabbit-nibbled pasture, is riddled with burrows between bumpy hummocks of thrift, which, as the soporific haze of the day drew on, beckoned with soft rolling cushions. The first part of the walk took us slightly inland past the only building on the island. The farmhouse is now the base for the nature reserve which has been here since 1959. We then took an anti-clockwise direction close to the cliff edges.

On our way to the northernmost point of the island, overlooking a lonely slab of rock known as Garland Stone, we were acclimatising ourselves to the sights, scents and sounds of the place. Although there are no land predators, black-backed gulls and ravens feast on the shearwater chicks. The adult shearwaters only return at night. Many chicks fall victim to these pirates and the visceral remains of shearwater chicks were strewn like a massacre scene almost everywhere. They are a modest-looking bird, sooty-brown above and white on all underparts, with long wings for their small size of about 30 cm in length. The chicks reach an impressive size, larger than their parents. They are fattened up and then deserted for the last two weeks of their young life on land, after which they take to the sky and will then fly, unescorted, the 7,000 miles to their next home on the east coast of South America. There were ravens in the sky all the time, black as doom, wheeling and croaking loudly. Ravens also breed here. I've seen ravens in these numbers before in Iceland. I found the island light, the cliffs, the windswept sea, the ravens, and the savagely tough grass to be reminiscent of that volcanic land.

We followed the path around the western curve of the island. There is evidence here of much older settlements, the dying bracken beginning to lie flat, exposing ancient sites that are prehistoric. Aerial photographic and laser scanning surveys have shown ancient fields systems and ritual monuments from the Bronze Age.

We stood at Skomer Head looking southeast towards Skokholm, the sun behind us, the breeze on our bare shoulders evaporating the moisture built up from the walk and slowly withdrawing the heat. A migrating flock of swallows made a straight line over us and out to sea with obvious intent. A flock of distant shearwater were settling into a huge raft, tiny dots in the muted flashing sea beyond the lofty cliffs below us, waiting for the safety of nightfall to return to their chicks and burrows. Looking out to the horizon, obscured by the haze, felt like standing at the threshold of another world. It was a defining moment; there was no past and no present; no sadness and no regrets; there was no fear of the future and there was no euphoria. Only the here and now. There was silent acknowledgement between us of the stillness of that moment.

✵

The penultimate part of the circumnavigation took us into The Wick, an inlet, where from one side we look directly over the cliff face on which thousands of nesting birds were defending the remaining unfledged chicks. With the aid of Mark's 8x40 mm binoculars, we could see guillemots, razorbills, kittiwakes, and fulmars. The guano streaked the rocks like spilt paint.

We met up with some of the reserve staff at the landing steps where they had gathered for an evening swim. Their conversation gave us a glimpse into their world. They were mainly in their twenties and all were here living away from home, enjoying a kind of remote expatriate life, sharing much, close to each other, not least their enthusiasm for the natural world and its preservation. One was shortly off to live on a reserve studying red squirrels and pine martens in Northumberland. Another had recently been assessing the conflict between human habitation and birds in North African marshes. They were an earnest group but were at ease at play in the evening sun, dipping into the cold clear water, chatting quietly.

Someone had recently dropped a camera into the deep water near the landing steps. Dave heroically offered to dive for it. The staff would be no match for Dave's competence in the water. He dug out his trunks from the kayak hatch and in no time his bulky shoulders were bobbing around the youngsters in the sea, not unlike the bull seal with his harem. He retrieved the camera with little effort.

Mark and I were enjoying the spectacle and the glinting water was winking and playing around the group. Then we noticed the bull seal, about a hundred metres away, slip off his isolated rock into the water. He seemed to be interested in the swimmers. One of the staff alerted the swimmers and suggested that they should all get out. Everyone except Dave made their way out and carefully hobbled across the weed-clad rocks to the steps. Dave had decided he wanted a proper swim and seemed to head off directly towards the enormous seal, which was at least 2 metres in length with a muscular thick neck. Mark looked at me and said, 'Do you think he doesn't know?'

My feelings swiftly changed from amusement to concern. Seals are territorial but tend to avoid human confrontation. It is not unknown however. 'Is this dangerous?' we yelled out, but Dave had his head down.

One of the girls who had come up to join us quietly said, 'He needs to get out now,' Mark pulled a Wallace and Gromit grin with no irony. Fortunately, Dave began to arc back towards us and the seal stopped, his whiskery rounded head stationary. Dave was none the wiser when he finally walked up the steps, drying his hair with a tea towel.

We spent an hour or so relaxing and chatting with the staff before we caught the optimum slack tide back to the mainland. We had more confidence for the return paddle, and it was our last time in the water for this trip. The crossing was safe and calm. We carried the kayaks up the hill to the truck, strapped the boats on the roof, bundled everything into the rear tray and set off to spend the evening in Dale, an unspoilt quiet village tucked into the south side of the peninsula.

We enjoyed a final debriefing of the day over beer and a hot meal, looking over the estuary to the twinkling lights of Milford Haven refinery. Tired and fed, we wandered out of the village, finding a level stone platform on top of some historic lime kilns to settle down upon for our final night. A distant fog horn signalled 'lights out'. I left the smell of damp moss and wet nettles in the dew of the descending night and buried my head into the breathing heat of my sleeping bag.

CRAB

CHAPTER 8

MEDWAY

The digital world is in your own hands

Das Boot – June 2022
We arrived at the 50-metre-long tapered cylinder of ragged and torn corroding steel lying in the mud like a discarded cigar twenty minutes before the tide was again to swallow it. What some researchers believe to be *SM UB-122* has lain here for over a hundred years in the extreme intertidal ecosystem of the Medway salt marshes. The timing of arrival is important and is a compromise between more time on the boat, or more mud to deal with.

This is not a war grave, and we were far from sombre. We hadn't been out together since the pandemic and we were in high spirits. We excitedly clambered carefully all over the wreck. The thick steel shell remains strong in most areas, but the whole thing was being reclaimed by nature and the steel plates were splintering like riven slate. The wheels, levers, cranks, and strange bowl shapes on the periphery of the interior had a look of disembowelment.

A leg through any of this would be a nasty business. We were careful. 'Blistering barnacles!' yelled Dave as a light touch of his knee against a serrated edge caused the familiar blood-speckled graze to seep bright red against the dried grey mud on his shin. Captain Haddock's description is quite accurate. The layers of barnacles were lifting and cracking away as the steel substrate billowed and blistered underneath.

The wreck didn't become visible to us until we were almost on it, because it lies low, with islands around it, and the route through the creek is a twisting one. The hulk lies in Humble Bee Creek up against a small island a few hundred metres offshore.

The prow has fallen away, and there is no conning tower or engine. The inside is just over half full with mud, but the structure is easily identifiable. The shape of the U-boat, means that the exterior steel plating has gradually started to fall apart. The several interior rib structures lay visible and decaying. Now with the matt bone-white coating of barnacles, the impression was much like the organic remains of a huge predator.

We had set off from The Strand in Gillingham, alongside the old Chatham Dockyard on the River Medway, slipping down Commodore's Hard into the muddy yellow waters. This is where Sir Francis Drake cut his maritime teeth – and where the Royal Navy were based – when Britain dominated the maritime world.

The industrial heritage of the area stretches back to Roman times when the woods of Kent provided the charcoal for iron works, and Kentish ragstone was transported up the Medway like a conveyor belt of ships to build Londinium. The dockyard, which built Nelson's *Victory*, slipped into decline over the second half of the twentieth century, but huge oil refineries and power stations were built nearby at Kingsnorth and on the Isle of Grain.

There is a modern gas-fuelled power station remaining at Kingsnorth, clearly visible from where we were, but most of the industry and shipping has withdrawn, leaving behind their skeletal remains in concrete, steel, and timber. We had slipped under the rickety supports of a disused pier just before turning down the creek to our destination. This dilapidated structure supports a few corroding pipelines that once gushed with crude oil from the Middle East to the BP refinery at Kingsnorth, and was at one time the longest pier in the world.

The Medway landscape is a dynamic one. Mud banks shift and change over time. High tide and low tide are like before and after some apocalyptic disaster. As the tide recedes, leaving miles of mud, only the narrow deep channels remain. Chains draped in inky seaweed and green slime swing forlornly under silent disused steel piers and landing berths, where buddleia sprout between corkscrew conveyors, once noisy and filthy with coal. The wind calls through lofty obsolete cranes, loose parts clanking, reaching out to sea with no work to do. The barnacles, limpets and mussels gradually replace the rusting steel between the tidal extremes. Huge timber supports, forgiving in texture to steel hulls, sourced from irreplaceable exotic forests, grow hollow and wait to be consumed by the mud. Near our destination, the long pier, derelict and falling into the silt, is laden with ramshackle, unsecured old pipe work, like the carrion entrails of a slain beast.

It had been a two-hour paddle to our U-boat. Nearby we had disturbed a colony of seals, which rushed in lolloping motion across the mud to the safety of the water where they found confidence to acknowledge their curiosity. Now they were appearing and disappearing constantly around our kayaks. We saw and heard substantial-sized fish around us, which presumably fed these fat furry mammals. There were plovers and turnstones, sandpipers and many oystercatchers. We paddled close to an avocet that was stalking along in a few inches of water, frantically working its upturned bill back and forth in the mud. This would have been a very rare sight only a few years ago.

We hauled our boats onto the tiny island and sat in the breeze eating Twiglets and sandwiches, contemplating what we surveyed. '*Das Boot!*' was cried out randomly all day long, but for a while we were in earnest thought. A U-boat is a killing machine. It sinks ships and takes life. The First World War was a time of death, and these vessels played their role with German efficiency. It was a

U-boat that sank RMS *Lusitania* in 1915, with the loss of many US citizens. As a response to resumed U-boat attacks on US merchant shipping, Woodrow Wilson finally brought his country to war with Germany in 1917. By the end of the war, U-boats had sunk 5,000 ships and taken 15,000 lives.

We grimaced at the thought of working on board the U-boat. It had a complement of thirty-one crew and three officers. Looking at the half-metre-width round bulkhead access ports, I pointed out they were more for Mark than Dave or me. It was claustrophobic thinking about it. 'You wouldn't want a lot of curry on board,' Mark pointed out, looking at the single toilet. The thought of being under depth charge attack in a metal coffin was terrifying.

This U-boat, I understand, commissioned in March 1918, surrendered at Harwich among a two-mile-long convoy of over a hundred other U-boats on 20 November of that year. A total of 160 U-boats surrendered at Harwich. The engine was removed and used in a cement works in Essex. I hadn't considered the implications of a diesel engine on a submersible vessel, but obviously it can't function when the boat is submerged. A submarine uses battery power. Cell phone technology has miniaturised battery size, but at the time of this submersible, the rechargeable batteries took up sixteen percent of the displacement space. It is assumed that SM *UB-122* broke from its mooring in the Medway while waiting to be scrapped at Chatham. The potential salvage costs meant that it has stayed here ever since.

We left with enough incoming tide to make the return trip an easy one. There is a fort on each of two small islands that we cruised between before the main conurbation of Gillingham. The Medway has always held strategic importance and since the Elizabethan rise of the dockyards, the channel has seen many forms of defence. These forts were completed by 1879 in response to political turmoil in Europe. It is argued that Britain's extravagant defence spending from the 1850s was a considerable deterrent factor resulting in the lack of invasion attempt up until the First World War. These forts were difficult to build and never saw any action. They were used as observation posts only during the two world wars.

We landed on the southernmost of the islands to explore Hoo Fort. We lifted our boats out among a few wrecked barges that were heaped against each other like hurricane damage left to rot. A chequerboard-tiled floor of a small shower on one of these barges, hoisted high and at an alarming angle, looked like bomb damage and reminded us that people lived and worked on these craft. The elegant curved timber hulls have sculptural beauty and the rufus hue of hefty iron fixings decorate the surface with a pleasing regular pattern.

We had heard a cuckoo on the way to the U-boat and when we landed, we disturbed its peace and watched its distinctive hawk-like wings and magpie-like long tail as it flew off the island.

The shingle was a mix of industrial waste, brick chipping and shell. Walking on the salty robust plant life just above the tide line, a pleasant odour drifted in the air. This contrasted with the methane stink of the grey mud, to which we had become accustomed. Sea purslane sprawled along most of these margins. With all of us in shorts, the thick border of brambles and nettles made it difficult to reach the circular fort that took up most of the island just a few metres higher.

We made our way through the obstacles and to our surprise found that someone had thoughtfully left an aluminium ladder on this surrounding low ground, almost like a moat, giving us access to the upper floor. We climbed up and entered the building through one of the gun placements apertures. The building is of large granite block with brick lining and vaulted roofs. We stepped over fifteen-inch-thick iron plate. These ten-foot by ten-foot plates infilling between the granite were built in the manner of contemporary ship gun defences and had timber linings to soften impact shock, and rope netting lining to protect the gunners from splintered timber.

There is little graffiti, and the basic structure looks to be in sound condition. Massive iron fixings remain here and there. The fireplaces on the lower-level quarters appear whole, with only floorboards and timber partitions missing from the ring of rooms that follows the circular layout.

Calm conditions prevailed for our last hop across the water back to The Strand.

※

Deadman's Island – *June 2023*

We were later to make another day trip on the Medway when we met up early one June morning at Queenborough on Sheppey, as we wanted to explore some of the other islands.

Mud is a major feature here, as everywhere in the estuary, but there is a long concrete slipway that enabled us to reach the low tide when we'd planned to start. We began with a sprint south and around Long Reach into a spot called Ladies Hole, which forms a U-bend in the waterway, in order to test paddling back into the wind. Returning to face the Medway, we assessed it as at our maximum wind strength. The wind was predicted to be 20 mph by lunchtime, which was higher than we would want. If we paddled southwest down the Medway, then the return would be against the tide but also right into the northeast wind, so we had a fallback plan to continue and land, then taxi back, instead of attempting to paddle back to our vehicle.

Our first stop was on Deadman's Island, a small flat mudbank with a few small shell beach mounds riddled with smaller channels and covered with sea purslane. The island is just half a mile from Queenborough and is a known gravesite. The Medway prison hulks of the eighteenth and nineteenth centuries often suffered outbreaks of disease and many inmates would have been lost. Some of these prisoners were buried on the island, and that gave its name. Coastal erosion, rising sea levels and the shifting nature of the muddy islands caused dismantled coffins, once six feet under, to appear on the surface. In 2016, the remains of two hundred souls were found here. There is a local tale of a black red-eyed dog that eats people and spits their bones into the sea. Dave thinks that the demon probably only wants to belong, like any dog. He wasn't going to scare us off.

The tide was incoming and it was a challenge finding a place to beach without deep mud, but we did find a shell bank just solid enough to take our weight. There were nests everywhere, so we wanted to avoid disturbing these. The wind was rising as we sat drinking hot tea from Dave's Thermos, looking over towards the cranes of Sheerness Docks. A huge bright red tanker was entering the estuary and being manoeuvred by a sturdy blue tug. It was absurdly long for the remaining channel with the tide still low.

We had seen images from someone's 2017 trip here, featuring gruesome skulls and coffins lying in the silt. We did find one bone, but it felt intrusive and voyeuristic and we were worried about the nests. There is tragedy in the history of these bones: French men and boys from Napoleonic wars; American prisoners from wars of independence; English petty criminals with poverty often allowing them no choice. The remains of all these are here. We slid back into the boats and set off, our legs now stinking and wet.

We bashed on as the tailwind began to rise, making the water choppy, and speeding progress. We soon took a course south, and then east, to land on the south side of Burntwick Island, where there are the remnants of an old pier. Until very recently, a colony of 1,200 pairs of sandwich terns nested here. With only 12,000 in the whole country, it was an important site. In lockdown, someone spent a night in the middle of their colony and the terns abandoned the island. We needed to be mindful of this.

The island is steadily disappearing underwater. Already most of it is submerged at high tide. It was used as a dump in Victorian times, and the landmass seems to be made largely of old bottles and crockery. We weren't going to stray far, because of the nesting, but we did gingerly make our way to the single stunted elder tree. There was a greylag goose nest at the elder's base, and (we thought appropriate) a chick-filled 'crow's nest' in the branches.

The island has been used as a quarantine base for ships infected by disease in past centuries, and like most islands, it has a smuggling heritage. There is just one derelict Second World War building remaining and it is usually part submerged. The forlorn and abandoned nature of the island has at least proved to benefit nesting birds. I brought back a ceramic white elephant as a souvenir. Presumably dumped among the rubbish in the nineteenth century, it has three legs and no trunk, but now happily stares out from among fig trees in my greenhouse.

We made a token effort to return to Queenborough, but we were heading, as we knew we would be, against the tide and wind with bows lifting and crashing down heavily into the waves. We took to plan B and paddled towards Lower Halstow with the wind behind us.

The scattered flat islands take on a fractured appearance, like ice flows in a warming sea, with food-rich mud banks stretching for mile upon mile. We saw common terns and little terns, egrets, and gulls. We saw two birds with a particular hard whiteness to them. Avocets were frequent now and seemed to allow us to approach quite close. We also saw sandwich terns, identifiable largely by the peculiar whiteness of their underparts. If you thought the more common gulls were white, these birds make them look cream in comparison.

This route followed a southward direction along the edge of a marshy peninsula. We'd moved to a quiet meditative mode of paddle now. On these stretches you find the steadiness of the long-distance runner. Your mind blanks. In a world where your digital life is removed from nature, you are reminded, as your hands and ten fingers rhythmically work your paddle, propelling yourself by your own exertion, that here, quite literally, the digital world is in your own hands.

The sea is changing the coastline all the time, but here we paddled past haphazard sea defences along a three-mile stretch where all manner of concrete waste has been bulldozed into the mud, forming a low artificial cliff edge of hard industrial waste. Dripping with cables and seaweeds, it was like some war zone barrier, which, you could say, is what it is. One area was made up of just toilet pans and cisterns, whose glossy surfaces resisted the adherence of seaweed. Not a tourist sight of choice, but the windswept abandon of the landscape here is the key attraction, even more astonishing due to its proximity to the metropolis.

The tide was receding fast and we wanted to avoid a tedious trudge through the mud, so the race was on to arrive before the tide exposed it all. We could see a timber jetty with a slipway with water still lapping its edges. We arrived with a depth of just six inches. We clambered onto the end of the slipway and pulled the boats up. This was the local yacht club, but everyone here was very friendly and offered us tea and a picnic table. We glanced back at the sea after five or six minutes to see that the water had vanished and mud was already stretching for hundreds of metres. We had just made it in time.

※

Lower Halstow is an ancient settlement. It has a beautiful old church and a tiny but historic creek-side wharf where Thames barges are usually moored. The motley crew of enthusiasts working on their boats in the boatyard told us that a 2017 Hollywood film, *Wonder Woman* had used this area as a location. This is an unlikely place to come across an American superhero.

There has, at least throughout my lifetime, been an air of urban poverty in the Medway towns, but house prices are very low for a place just 30 miles from Central London. The whole area is part of the Thames Gateway development scheme and billions of pounds of investment has just started to pour into the area. The people of Sheppey have an island mentality but their prosperity will always be linked to the Medway towns. The people on mainland Medway are diverse and multicultural, like Londoners. The metropolis will have ever greater influence here. With luck, some of its wealth will arrive by osmosis. The marshes and seashore in the Medway area of the North Kent coast have no attractive sandy beaches and offer little easy swimming access. There are no holiday seaside features. The Hoo Peninsula, and the muddy creeks and tussocky islands of the area, where it is assumed Dickens based some of his most memorable characters, is a special environment. The *Great Expectation* should be that this area will remain a windswept wilderness, and the extensive naval and industrial heritage will be appreciated by future generations.

CHAPTER 9

AND ONE FOR ALL

Cast your dreams to the morning sky; the evening arrives soon enough

The health of English and Welsh rivers has deteriorated during the course of these adventures. Water companies have received deserved condemnation for polluting our waterways, and sewage filth is a headline grabber. Private equity and shareholders' dividends were always likely to restrict capital investment. What is the logical conclusion of this? If good air quality eventually becomes scarce – and it needs industrial-scale investment to make it safe – would we be happy to see the air we all breathe sold off and privatised? Scottish rivers have much smaller problems, and it is surely no coincidence that Scottish Water is publicly run. Modern farming is an even greater culprit. The Wye, in particular, has suffered because of the vast expansion of chicken farming nearby and the subsequent runoff of nutrients when chicken manure is spread on the land. Currently the Thames, the Wye and the Medway are all much cleaner now than at other times in their history, but if we value their place in our society, then we must fight to improve them.

In March 2023, the Vjosa Wild River National Park was finally designated in a ceremony at Tepelenë, thus ensuring the preservation of the ecosystem as a living free-flowing river for the benefit of the local population and the surrounding natural habitat.

Steve Feltham is still looking for his monster. The dolphins at Chanonry Point are thriving. Scotland has more than half of Britain's Marine Protected Areas.

Skomer, Skokholm and the Marloes Peninsula in Pembrokeshire is a Marine Conservation Zone and remains in good health. The colonies of Manx shearwater, puffin, and lesser black-backed gulls have generally been doing well. Bird flu in 2022, however, has caused a major threat to Britain's sea birds. The population of northern gannets on Grassholme has been reduced by a staggering 50 percent. Guillemots and razorbills have also been hard hit. It will be a long recovery from this.

The River Rats have every intention of continuing their journeys as long as age and health will allow. A comment from Dave in one of our many planning emails when he had recently returned from working at the In Flanders Fields Museum in Belgium was that if he were in the trenches, he would like to have Mark and me alongside him. He and Mark have been alongside me in the trenches all along. I'm thankful for that.

Every generation bemoans the passing of the world they knew. The ever-present evils of war and persistent poverty are major drivers of environmental disaster, but climate change now trumps all other problems. The world, however, still groans under the weight of its own beauty. Experiencing outdoor pleasures in the way we did when it was all new to us, with a young heart and innocent optimism, will bring rejuvenation where there is cynicism. We will always gather commitments and surfeit clutter in our lives, but finding space to flood your senses with this beauty is a treasure that is free to all.

Cast your dreams to the morning sky; the evening arrives soon enough.

CHAPTER 9 — AND ONE FOR ALL

THE RAT PACK

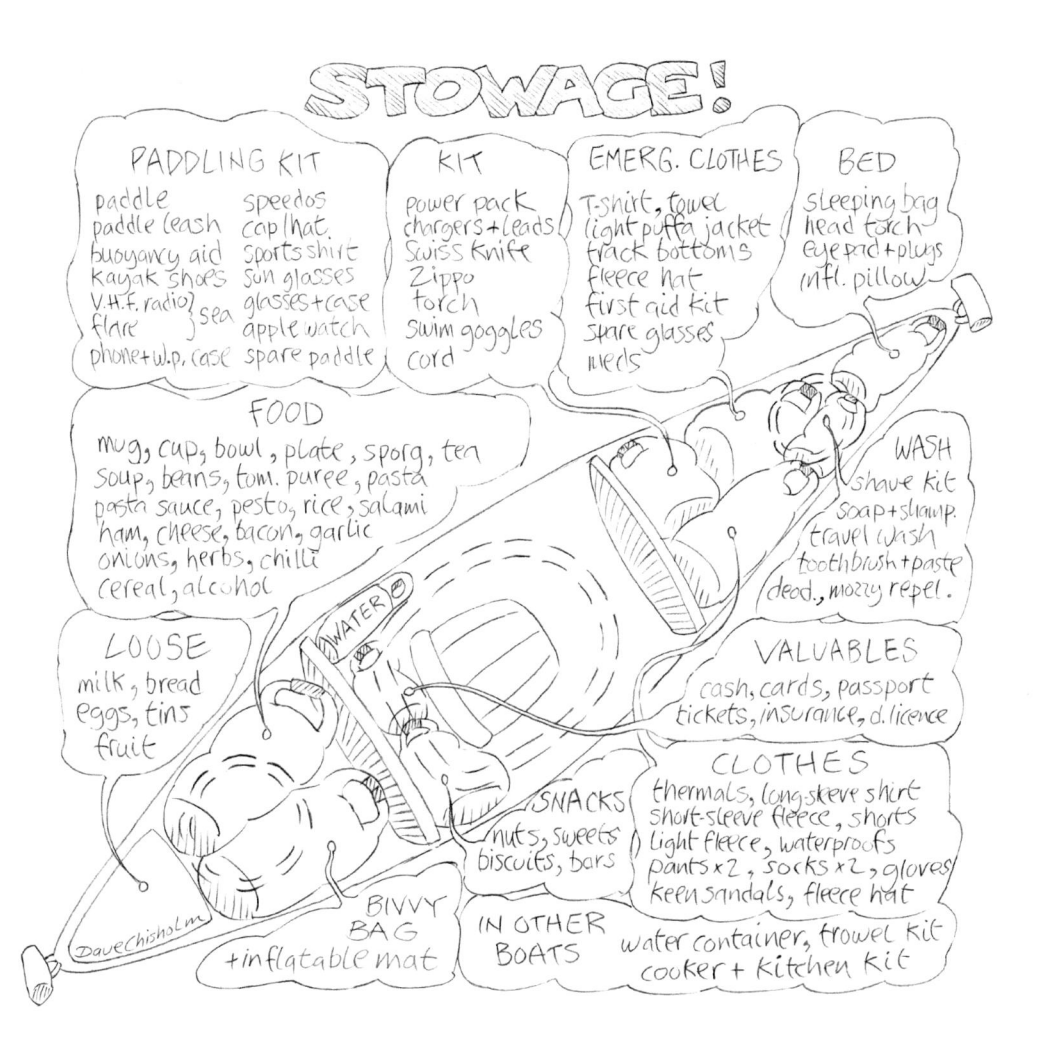

STOWAGE!

PADDLING KIT
paddle
paddle leash
buoyancy aid
kayak shoes
V.H.F. radio
flare
phone + w.p. case
speedos
cap/hat
sports shirt
sun glasses
sea glasses + case
apple watch
spare paddle

KIT
power pack
chargers + leads
Swiss knife
Zippo
torch
swim goggles
cord

EMERG. CLOTHES
T-shirt, towel
light puffa jacket
track bottoms
fleece hat
first aid kit
spare glasses
meds

BED
sleeping bag
head torch
eye pad + plugs
infl. pillow

FOOD
mug, cup, bowl, plate, sporg, ten
soup, beans, tom. puree, pasta
pasta sauce, pesto, rice, salami
ham, cheese, bacon, garlic
onions, herbs, chilli
cereal, alcohol

WASH
shave kit
soap + shamp.
travel wash
toothbrush + paste
deod., mozzy repel.

LOOSE
milk, bread
eggs, tins
fruit

WATER

VALUABLES
cash, cards, passport
tickets, insurance, d. licence

SNACKS
nuts, sweets
biscuits, bars

CLOTHES
thermals, long-sleeve shirt
short-sleeve fleece, shorts
light fleece, waterproofs
pants x 2, socks x 2, gloves
keen sandals, fleece hat

BIVVY BAG
+ inflatable mat

IN OTHER BOATS
water container, trowel kit
cooker + kitchen kit

Dave Chisholm

203

ABOUT THE AUTHOR

Nick lives in the countryside of the North Downs in East Kent.

He has run an assortment of businesses over the years focussing on the preservation of historic buildings. He has also worked as a sculptor and a scenic painter.

He is a dedicated grower of food and can often be found settled in among the tomatoes and grapes in his greenhouse where he will write.

River Ratting is Nick's first book.

.